BANKING ON DIGITAL GROWTH

BANKING

—— ON ——

DIGITAL GROWTH

THE STRATEGIC MARKETING MANIFESTO TO TRANSFORM FINANCIAL BRANDS

JAMES ROBERT LAY

LIONCREST
PUBLISHING

BANKING ON DIGITAL GROWTH
The Strategic Marketing Manifesto to Transform Financial Brands

ISBN   978-1-5445-0772-9 *Hardcover*
       978-1-5445-0771-2 *Paperback*
       978-1-5445-0770-5 *Ebook*

For my wife Delena, you truly are my helpful and empathetic guide.

CONTENTS

A NOTE ON TERMINOLOGY

Before we get started, I believe it is important to address the problem of defining—or at least aligning around a common definition of—what *digital growth* actually means. It's clear, from the initial diagnostic work my team and I do with financial brands, the majority of bank and credit union leadership teams don't truly understand the concept.

When we begin talking to them about digital, they often latch on to terms like "online banking" and "mobile banking." In other words, they're thinking about the *delivery* of the banking services and all the service-oriented pieces of the business model.

But that's *not* what we're looking at in this book—and when I say, "digital growth," I'm referring not to the delivery model but the growth model, built on growth activities like marketing and sales.

This book defines digital growth as a systematic process, centered on the modern consumer journey, that unites marketing, sales, operations, and IT teams around the following goals: (a) increasing website traffic, (b) generating and nurturing leads, and (c) converting those leads into loans and deposits.

Digital growth positions a financial brand *beyond* the commoditized great rates, amazing service, and laundry lists of look-alike bullet-point product features that every other financial institution promotes.

It is important to note early and often that digital growth takes time. I liken it to running a marathon, and even that is not a perfect metaphor, because there's no finish line when it comes to digital growth. In fact, digital growth has no end because as you move forward and make progress, you will always discover new roadblocks to eliminate in addition to new opportunities to create or capture.

Digital growth is a journey—a journey from good to great.

INTRODUCTION

CONSUMERS HAVE CHANGED—HAVE YOU?

Money is stressful.

According to a recent study conducted by Northwestern Mutual, 85 percent of Americans today feel stress about their finances.

And it's only getting worse. From soaring housing costs to the student loan crisis, financial anxiety is real—and it's taking a significant toll on people's health, relationships, and overall sense of well-being.

What does this mean for you and your financial brand?

The reality is, in this modern economic climate, consumers have changed. They simply don't trust financial institutions like they used to. Financial brands who don't adapt to these new consumer attitudes and don't adjust their marketing and sales strategies to reflect and address consumer financial stress will find themselves at grave risk.

Unfortunately, this is exactly what's happening almost across the board among traditional banks and credit unions. Rather than welcoming the opportunity to fill a new need—with modern messaging and communication strategies that speak to those (particularly millennials and younger) desperately looking for a partner they can *trust*, who can guide them to a bigger, better, and brighter future—most financial brands are still doing the same old marketing they always have, in the same way they always have.

Moreover, their marketing and sales strategies don't reflect the way consumer *behavior* has changed. In today's digital world, consumers are empowered with unlimited access to knowledge and information. They also have more available options than ever before to consider. They do their own research on their own time before making any decisions.

Digital has changed the way people shop, and we also see that in how they buy financial services. Consumers are coming into branches less and less. But financial institutions are still stuck in an outdated, branch-first growth model, where in-person branch visits are seen as primary selling opportunities. The truth of the matter is, even when folks *do* come into branches nowadays (if they come into a branch at all), most of the time their buying decisions have already been made long before—at a much earlier stage in the consumer journey.

If you're like many of the banks and credit unions I've worked with, you *know* your financial brand's future growth is not going to come from branches alone—if from branches *at all*. You've watched branch traffic decline year after year.

You may also have struggled when it comes to your marketing efforts, as you've only *dabbled in digital*. You might have built a mobile-responsive, ADA-compliant website, sent emails, placed digital ads, and posted content on social media. But you feel stuck, and deep down you know why: traditional broadcast marketing strategies and tactics do not work with digital marketing. How could they? You know as well as I do every financial brand is out there promoting the same commoditized great rates, amazing service, and laundry lists of look-alike bullet-point product features.

What's the solution?

How are you going to finally transform your marketing and sales strategies for a digital-first economy, maximize your growth, and rocket ahead of your competitors?

First, you need to see this revolution for what it is and embrace it—not fear it.

THE FOURTH INDUSTRIAL REVOLUTION

There have been three past Industrial Revolutions, and we are now in the midst of a fourth—a concept that Klaus Schwab, founder and executive chair of the World Economic Forum and author of *The Fourth Industrial Revolution*—is well known for shaping. First, of course, was the steam revolution of the late 1700s, then the electric revolution of the late 1800s, and finally the computer revolution of the 1960s and '70s. Not as often discussed, however, are the revolutions in marketing that accompanied these developments, from print (newspapers) to mass media (TV and radio) to digital (internet).

With the fourth Industrial Revolution, we have now, in the 2010s, moved beyond the computer age and entered a new era of exponential technologies such as robotics, artificial intelligence (AI), virtual reality (VR), the internet of things (IoT), and more.

What does this mean for the evolution of marketing?

With the rise of automation comes the new potential for one-to-one consumer communication strategies *at scale*. The old days of one-to-many messaging are dead and gone. That kind of one-way, broadcast marketing is simply no longer relevant. The name of the game now is reaching people where they are, along the course of their own consumer journey, so you can communicate and build connection through **empathy**—with digital relationships that put *them* first.

> Just as we are in the fourth revolution in technology, we are also in the fourth revolution in marketing.

Throughout this book, we will return to these concepts of empathy and the consumer journey. Every one of us is on a journey. Narrative is central to human existence, but as we will learn in the following chapters, *there can be only one hero in every story.*

Consumers are not looking for a hero. Consumers *are* the hero.

When you put the consumer and their hero's journey at the heart of everything you do—when you take an empathetic approach to marketing and sales—it is truly transformative. In today's digital world, it is precisely these "soft skills" of empathy and emotional intelligence that constitute real competitive advantage for financial brands.

You need that advantage more than ever, as there are now more and more financial brands and fintechs entering the marketplace whose business models are built specifically around a digital- and mobile-first growth strategy. These neobanks and digital lenders are transforming the entire industry. They're already capturing market share from traditional banks and credit unions, and the truth is, many of these legacy institutions will cease to exist in the next ten to twenty years.

You've come to this book because you are part of a financial brand marketing, sales, or leadership team that wants to be one of the winners in this new digital economy. You want to see your financial brand's loans and deposits continue to grow. And although you've made efforts to move forward and make progress along your own Digital Growth Journey, you haven't seen the results you had hoped for.

Why not?

THE FOUR FEARS

Up to this point, you've only dabbled in digital. You've done everything you know how to do. But you're not sure what comes next. You feel stuck, and you don't quite know why. You *want* to find a better path forward. You see the writing on the wall: the changes in technology, consumer behavior, and competition in the financial marketplace.

But there is something preventing you and your marketing team from realizing your digital growth potential. Legacy systems and thinking that were put in place long before you got to where you are today threaten to hold you back.

What exactly are these hidden forces at play?

Having worked with hundreds of financial brands and their marketing teams, I've seen how they can get trapped in what I call the **Circle of Chaos**, as they try to navigate their way through these intricate environmental changes happening around technology, consumers, and the competition.

It's easy to feel confused, frustrated, and overwhelmed as digital continues to transform the world at an exponential pace. Working to maximize your financial brand's digital growth can sometimes feel like an impossible feat.

But when you examine the Circle of Chaos a little more closely, you see this condition is rooted in fear. Financial brands are held back by four distinct fears keeping them from fully committing to their Digital Growth Journey. These are sometimes spoken openly, but more often than not, they are whispered in confidence. They are:

1. **Fear of the unknown** ("I know digital is important for us, but what should we do next?")

2. **Fear of change** ("Why change now? We have had success up to this point.")

3. **Fear of failure** ("What happens if we try this and fail? What will they think of me?")

4. **Fear of success** ("What happens if this actually *works*? Can we even support this new type of growth?")

5. What about you? Are you stuck in the Circle of Chaos? How can you escape it?

> Are your fears holding you back from maximizing your financial brand's future growth potential?

10X THINKING

It doesn't make matters any easier that financial brand marketing teams are greatly misunderstood and undervalued.

Marketing departments are typically viewed as nothing more than cost centers, or worse, a bunch of grown-up kids who play with paint and crayons all day long—**glorified in-house FedEx Kinko's stores that exist just to take orders and serve the last-minute needs of others.**

What if this disparaging image was turned on its head? What if your marketing team stopped feeling like overwhelmed and frustrated order takers and instead became the strategic growth leader within your financial brand?

What if instead of taking marketing for granted, your sales and leadership teams saw marketing as the trusted vehicle to drive your financial brand toward a future of exponential digital growth? What if instead of being viewed as a necessary evil or cost center, marketing finally *proves* its value by generating 10X more loans and deposits?

I'm not exaggerating when I say 10X growth is totally doable. It's important to me people understand this. I've seen this level of growth firsthand, over and over again. In fact, I've seen financial brands experience 15X digital growth! Yes, this is a book about saving financial brands from extinction with digital growth, but it's not just about surviving—it's about thriving. And the way to do this is through 10X thinking.

As Dan Sullivan of Strategic Coach shares, lots of people can 2X something, make it twice as good. They can work longer and harder, they can throw more dollars at the problem. But **if you really want exponential digital growth—which is what is needed for financial brands—you're going to have to transform your entire way of thinking, your marketing and sales strategic models, and all the habits that go along with it.**

How do you do this? By using the Digital Growth Blueprint.

BANKING ON PURPOSE WITH THE DIGITAL GROWTH BLUEPRINT

Digital growth is a journey—a journey from good to great.

It is a journey that begins in the *mind*. Marketing, sales, and leadership teams at financial brands must first transform their thinking—only then can they transform themselves, their teams, and their strategies for exponential future digital growth.

It doesn't happen overnight. Like running a marathon, it all starts with proper training and planning. Then, once you are off and running, you have to be open to changing conditions, as the environment is unpredictable.

The Digital Growth Blueprint and strategic marketing manifesto I put forth in this book is made up of twelve key areas.

They **build on each other but are also independent.** In other words, even if you focus on and commit to only one of these twelve points of the manifesto, this effort alone can empower you to make your financial brand's marketing even better. And if you focus on all twelve, you transform your *entire* financial brand to maximize your future digital growth potential.

THE DIGITAL **GROWTH** STRATEGIC MARKETING MANIFESTO

WE WILL POSITION PRODUCTS BEYOND BULLET POINTS	WE WILL BUILD A WEBSITE THAT SELLS	WE WILL PROVE MARKETING'S VALUE ONCE AND FOR ALL
WE WILL EMPATHIZE WITH CONSUMER PERSONAS	WE WILL MAXIMIZE MARKETING TECHNOLOGIES	WE WILL PROMOTE CONTENT ONLY TO GUIDE PEOPLE
WE WILL DEFINE A DIGITAL GROWTH PURPOSE	WE WILL MAP OUT DIGITAL CONSUMER JOURNEYS	WE WILL PRODUCE CONTENT THAT HELPS FIRST
WE WILL LEARN FROM THE PAST TO ESCAPE THE PRESENT	WE WILL ESCAPE THE DANGERS OF DOING DIGITAL	WE WILL BE THE HELPFUL AND EMPATHETIC GUIDE
ESTABLISH A STRONG FOUNDATION FOR DIGITAL GROWTH	**BUILD A DIGITAL GROWTH ENGINE**	**MAXIMIZE YOUR DIGITAL GROWTH POTENTIAL**

Unfortunately, the majority of banks and credits unions are nowhere close to this. Through our year-over-year research, we continue to find an ever-growing divide—following the Pareto principle, aka the 80/20 rule, with the minority (20%) of financial brands becoming the "digital haves" while the majority (80%) of banks and credit unions, the "digital have-nots," struggle to transform themselves for digital growth.

Why are the 80 percent having such trouble?

Digital growth requires much more than just adopting the latest and greatest marketing and sales technology. In fact, one of the most important elements of digital growth is something ancient and timeless but often left out of the conversation altogether: Humanity. People.

We're not robots...yet.

People still trust *people*—far more than they do financial brands. There's something about connecting with another human being that makes consumers feel good, and it's especially important for you and your team, because of the nature of financial services and its inherent complexity. This human connection can happen online—through a chat or even something like Face-Time or Zoom—or it can be face-to-face. What matters isn't the channel of connection but the connection of humanity.

Branches may not be disappearing entirely (yet), but they are no longer the transactional center for deposits, transfers, payments, and the like, that they were in the past. Instead, in today's digital economy, branches will become centers for financial coaching, guidance, and accountability, physical places for your financial brand to provide deep-level in-person expertise—all of which will support your new digital-first growth model.

Again, consumers don't want to hear you brag about your commoditized rates, service, and features. Rather, they want to feel you *get* them on every level of their life.

Here lies one of the greatest opportunities for your financial brand.

Use the Digital Growth Blueprint to **define your purpose, one that transcends dollars and cents**. Then, communicate and fulfill that purpose with digital growth strategies that educate, empower, and elevate consumers beyond their financial stress. Provide them with helpful content and experiences that guide them toward a bigger, better, and brighter future.

Through the following chapters detailing this strategic marketing manifesto, I will show you exactly how to do this: first, by establishing a strong *foundation* for digital growth; then, building the Digital Growth Engine that will drive your new digital-first/mobile-first strategic marketing and sales model; and finally, maximizing your digital growth potential to generate 10X more loans and deposits.

Digital growth is a *journey*.

You won't get there right away. But if you follow this framework, you will begin to see progress almost immediately. Don't get distracted or lose hope when you want to fall back on old patterns and behaviors that feel safe. Keep your eyes on creating a bigger, better, and brighter future for yourself, your team, and the people in the communities your financial brand serves. Forget about perfection and focus on the progress you make day after day, week after week, and month after month.

Before long, you and your team will gain a newfound clarity. You will build courage and commitment, and your confidence will grow. Not only are you establishing new digital marketing systems, technologies, and habits that will transform your financial brand, but you are also letting go of the limiting mindsets, strategies, and behaviors that have been holding you back for so long.

Ultimately, **breaking free from legacy marketing and sales systems built around branches and broadcast** will lead you and your financial brand to an exciting future of exponential digital growth.

So enjoy the journey. But remember, it's a marathon, not a sprint.

The good news is, you don't have to run this race alone. I am here to help guide you along the way.

WHO AM I?

Over the past eighteen years, I've guided—along with my team at the Digital Growth Institute—more than 520 banks and credit unions. Our mission: to simplify digital marketing and sales strategies that empower financial brands to generate 10X more loans and deposits. Through training, research, and insights, along with strategic coaching, we've helped our clients transform their marketing and sales strategies, systems, technologies, and habits.

We are a purpose-driven organization, committed to educating, empowering, and elevating financial brands so they, in turn, can do the same to help the communities they serve. We know money is stressful. And we know today's consumers have a great deal of anxiety around their financial situations.

We also know banks and credit unions, including the key stake-holders and leadership teams within them, are often held back by the Four Fears, but it doesn't have to be that way. The time for action is now. I wrote this strategic marketing manifesto to educate, empower, and elevate you and your team to commit to move forward with courage and confidence as you make continued progress along your own Digital Growth Journey.

PART ONE

ESTABLISH
A STRONG
FOUNDATION FOR
DIGITAL GROWTH

When you're building a physical branch location for your financial brand, you don't just jump in and start pouring concrete. First, of course, you have to assess the situation, study consumer traffic patterns, and look at positioning in the local marketplace. You select your site, draw up blueprints, and more.

All in all, there's a lot of planning that goes into it; and like with anything you build, you need a strong structural foundation. Otherwise, your building will tumble and fall.

The same is true when it comes to your Digital Growth Journey. If you jump the gun and wind up too far ahead of yourself without a well-defined digital growth strategy, you'll end up right where you started: back in the Circle of Chaos feeling confused, frustrated, and overwhelmed!

Don't put the cart before the horse. **Before you dive into the doing of digital, it's important to take the time to focus on four key areas: learning from the past, defining your purpose, empathizing with consumer personas, and positioning your products beyond bullet points.**

Get these right and you will have a rock-solid foundation for digital growth!

* * * * *

CHAPTER ONE

WE WILL LEARN FROM THE PAST TO ESCAPE THE PRESENT

It's 2007. A man known for his jeans and black turtlenecks steps onto the stage and introduces his company's new product: the iPhone.

This revolutionary piece of technology combined three different tools in one. Yes, it was a *cellular phone*, but like his earlier breakthrough, the iPod, it was also a *music player*—and most transformative of all, an *internet communication device* (as it was called at the time), with email, web browsing, and more.

The moment this man stepped on that stage, it changed forever the way we communicate with one another.

Communication is at the heart of marketing and sales— and is the key to the future of growth for any financial brand.

It was only a dozen years ago Steve Jobs introduced the iPhone. Think of all the exponential changes we've experienced *since* that time. Not only has technology evolved at an exponential rate, but so have consumer expectations. Meanwhile, *competition*—to keep up with those technologies and the changing consumer demands around them—has gone through the roof.

Take, for example, the music industry. Certainly, there were changes already happening before 2007, but in retrospect, the iPhone might have been its death knell. Jobs's innovation sped up the rate of change enormously and on a macro scale.

This pattern can be seen across industries.

> The financial marketplace is being transformed and disrupted by changes in technology, consumer expectations, and the competition.

DIGITAL DISRUPTION

When any industry experiences disruption, as Peter Diamandis and Steven Kotler share in their book *Bold*, a series of six events occurs. As the authors explain, "The Six Ds are a chain reaction of technological progression, a road map of rapid development that always leads to enormous upheaval and opportunity."

I'd like to zoom in and focus on three of the six Ds: dematerialization, democratization, and demonetization.

Consider how the music industry has evolved from vinyl to eight-track to cassette to CD to MP3 and now streaming. Film followed a similar trajectory, from big reels to VHS to DVD to Netflix and so on.

Notice the shift from larger pieces of technology and media to smaller, and eventually to "nothing." Or at least nothing tangible in the physical world. With each shift, the new technology and media becomes a standardized part of the culture, the operating norm in society—and now **dematerialization** has become the norm.

In banking, we've seen dematerialization play out on multiple fronts but primarily up to this point on the transactional side of banking. For example, consumers have moved away from going to a physical branch to deposit checks and complete other transactional tasks. Instead, they use their mobile device to deposit checks digitally through an app.

Even the very concept of a *traditional check* is going through the dematerialization process, as peer-to-peer payment apps grow in popularity to replace physical payments. If you have young kids like me, you think it's great you can pay your babysitter with Zelle or Venmo or PayPal and don't have to worry about writing a check (or, worse, having no cash on hand and racing to make that extra ATM stop on the way home!).

Understandably, the dematerialization process makes those who've built their entire careers around the physical world of branch sales and broadcast marketing feel confused, frustrated, and overwhelmed about digital growth. No longer can they see, touch, or feel the world around them.

It can be **scary for people to see their physical world taken away from them before their very eyes.** I get it: like everything, digital comes with the perceived good and the bad.

Which brings us to the second part of digital disruption, which is **democratization.**

Let's go back to the example of the music industry. We know record labels and production houses *used to* control the entire process from front to back. They were the hitmakers and gate-keepers who pulled all the strings.

In contrast, we now have these digital platforms where total nobodies can strike a chord with a mass audience and become global pop stars. Certainly, without YouTube there would be no Justin Bieber. Whether that particular example resonates with you may depend on your musical taste, but he is just one example of many who have gained the capability to create and communicate directly with audiences through new technologies and distribution channels.

Likewise, we see streaming platforms like Netflix, Hulu, and Amazon Prime democratizing the film world by offering diverse options to many niche audiences. These companies are not traditional production studios, but they are now making their own content—and using the power of digital to serve a wider market than the old-school Hollywood entertainment giants.

Finally, as it relates to banking, we see democratization in the rise of financial brands with a digital- or mobile-first business model. Fintechs and neobanks are popping up left and right and by the thousands, communicating directly with and creating value directly *for* niche market segments through digital and mobile technologies.

Whether in banking or entertainment, digital has given

power to the people—the power to connect and communicate—at scale.

But again, not everyone thinks these changes are great, and where a lot of the discontent is felt is among those legacy brands who *used to* hold all the chips but are now being stripped of their power and control.

In particular, they are losing the power to control pricing and make money in the same way they always have. **Demonetization**, the third part of digital disruption, is a doozy. Record labels felt this pain in a big way. In the heyday of recorded music—I'm referring in this context to its modern era, at the peak of CD sales in the mid-'90s, before the bottom fell out—labels were raking it in, charging $15 to $20 per disc, with very low production costs. As it turns out, the consumer wanted only two or three songs on each release. But tough luck for them: the record companies controlled the pricing model and could do whatever they wished.

We all know what happened next. The rise of digital and broadband brought about a democratization of music, and this led to a radical shift in the industry's power balance. Labels lost their ability to set prices. No longer could they, essentially, set the terms for how listeners received and paid for music. The disruption from digital technology swept away a lot of the money—or rather, the particular legacy revenue streams and structures—that had previously been taken for granted.

At first, when Napster came on the scene, some predicted this demonetization would be virtually absolute, that listeners were simply never going to pay for recorded music again. I was in high school at the time and (I say this without any pride) was highly allergic to paying for music. In fact, I remember how I would fiendishly download music back then. Nonstop: I'm talking 24/7. My parents would be outside my bedroom door late at night, telling me to go to sleep or reprimanding me for always making our household's internet speed slow to a crawl.

But I wasn't just downloading music *for me*. As a young entrepreneur in the making (or budding criminal, depending on your point of view), I saw the possibilities in the new technology. I was one of the first kids in my school to get a DSL internet connection (128 Kbps, which was twice the speed of dial-up) and a CD burner. I would burn fully customized discs from songs off Napster, then sell them the next day for $10 each.

The kids at school loved it. Instead of having to schlep down to Best Buy or Target and drop $15 to $20 to buy a CD with only two or three tracks they actually liked, now for half the price they could get from me twenty of the hottest jams of 1999.

Youthful indiscretions aside, I bring up the story because it shows how I took advantage as an individual of these three crucial elements in digital disruption: dematerialization, democratization, and demonetization.

Of course, today, there wouldn't be the same appetite for those customized CDs. Nor, I would argue, is there the same consumer frustration. For the most part, we don't feel like we're being gouged anymore. We have much more say over how we want our personal entertainment dollar spent, and with streaming services we can pay $8 to $15 a month to unlock an entire library of music and movies.

Of course, demonetization, and digital disruption in general, is changing the whole model of banking, too.

What happened in music and film, those exact patterns, are very much coming into the banking space. Just like with those other industries, **the entire banking model up to this point has been built around the *physical* world**. Now everything is changing: the pricing models of the past, the way we even think about making money (i.e., net-interest income and non-interest income)—all of it.

Yet, for the most part, our industry remains trapped in digital denial.

DIGITAL DENIAL

We get trapped in digital denial when we are shortsighted and don't see the enormous digital growth potential for what it is. We try this or that but then give up because it doesn't yield results quick enough. Such a mistake. When *any* industry is transformed by disruption, inevitably the digital growth potential appears limited at first, deceptively so.

Value creation probably *is* going to lag out of the gate. In some cases, it might be nonexistent—or even appear as a tremendous up-front cost to establish new foundational systems, processes, and habits.

Don't be fooled. This is one of the deadliest blind spots but also the most common. What happens in digital denial is the leadership team within a financial brand mistakenly makes their most important decisions *based on the past*.

This is very understandable as these are folks, mind you, who have built their entire careers on past performance. Now, however, they're in a situation where they're stuck in the *present* moment. But they're making these strategic present-day decisions (around marketing, sales, and growth models) *rooted in* past perspectives and experiences and informed by earlier successes that are simply no longer relevant or useful anymore.

What do you think happens when they do that?

It depends. The results of their decisions may not be disastrous. They may well continue down a path of incremental linear growth. The trend lines will still nudge up. But that's it.

DIGITAL **GROWTH** VS LEGACY GROWTH

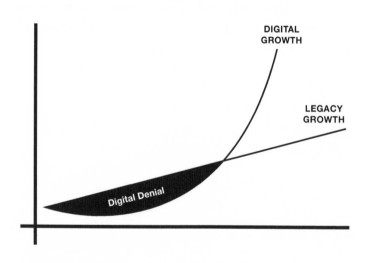

Notably, **they aren't taking advantage of the exponential growth curve that digital makes possible.**

In *digital* value creation, there is a deceptive doubling effect, again as Peter Diamandis and Steven Kotler note in their Six Ds model, where first digital appears to be a loss. But then, the value and growth generated by digital becomes twice as great, which then becomes four times as great, and so on. The doubling pattern continues until you reach a point where the digital growth becomes the primary driver and eventually crushes the old legacy growth model.

Look at Amazon, for example. According to TheStreet.com, without AWS and Prime membership, Amazon lost about $2 billion in Q1 of 2018.[1] This loss is directly rooted in the retail side of their business, which interestingly makes up 60 percent of their entire revenue model. Put another way, 60 percent of Amazon's total business operated at a loss. However, they greatly offset these losses through diverse digital revenue streams like AWS and Prime memberships. Amazon is doing the definition of *playing the long game*, which is the opposite of what we see among those risk-averse financial brand leaders who are looking at their situation in the present moment while being informed by past decisions.

Digital value creation has an incredible doubling effect.

---

1   TheStreet Guest Contributor, "Amazon Is Losing Billions from Its Retail Business and Rivals Should Be Scared," TheStreet, April 27, 2018, https://www.thestreet.com/opinion/amazon-is-losing-money-from-retail-operations-14571703.

ESCAPING THE PRESENT

When we're stuck in the present, we risk getting crushed and run over—never making it to the future. It's a **head-down versus head-up way of operating**. But unfortunately, it's typical of today's legacy leaders. They stay heads-down, trapped in the here and now, using the past as basis for their decision making, instead of heads-up, looking toward the future and seeing exponential change for what it is.

It's true of business leaders across the board in many industries. According to a recent report by Duke University, 97 percent of business leaders "believe strategy is important" and 96 percent don't feel like they "have the time to think strategically." How crazy is that!

Leaders of financial brands would be wise to buck this trend. Sure, bankers by default are going to be more risk-averse— that's what we do: we limit risks. But in this case, it may be that our limiting of risk *is* the actual risk that takes us under! Let's not let our strength become our greatest weakness or fatal flaw.

After all, we're lucky to have avoided much of the pain and misery that, for example, the music industry went through. We have had the luxury to learn from the failures of brands who have been down this journey and aren't with us today—retail stores like Blockbuster and Borders.

When it comes down to it, this is what legacy banks and credit unions *are* or have been historically—they're essentially retail or retail-like institutions built for the physical world. And as anyone who has read the news in recent years knows, the retail sector is in some trouble these days.

What these legacy retail brands lacked was leadership.

That is why a direct distinction between financial brand leadership and management must be drawn. Managers operate in the present moment to avoid risk and loss. On the other hand, those in leadership look ahead to create a future that does not yet exist.

One is not better than the other. Great leaders need great managers to apply their strategic thinking and ensure it becomes reality, while great managers need great leaders to ensure they don't get stuck in the present moment and make decisions informed by the past.

This isn't happening nearly enough, and it's one of my biggest concerns for financial brands in today's digital economy: the number of managers managing financial brands in the present moment far outweigh the number of leaders leading their financial brands with courage and confidence to create a bigger, better, and brighter future.

How, then, have financial brands not yet been decimated by digital disruption? For one, banking is a very different kind of consumer experience than listening to a song or watching a movie. The level of risk is obviously higher: they're trusting you with their life savings! But a lot of that risk is also just perception, and that perception is rapidly changing. Just think: it used to be that people were scared to use their credit card online. Now, of course, e-commerce is ubiquitous.

Still, perception is perception, and consumer research shows that when it comes to banking, people, including millennials, *do* still want to have a physical branch location (at least for now). It's not entirely logical: they'll do all their personal banking online, but they are reassured to know the physical branch is there. They'll say, "It's nice to see the building and think *that's* where I keep my money, even though I realize all my money isn't actually in there!"

Like I said, not totally logical. But emotions matter, and for whatever reason, this dynamic means—or at least it's partially responsible for the fact—that financial brands have been spared the kind of annihilating disruption other industries have faced.

It's also true government regulation has slowed the pace of disruption in the financial marketplace. But that is changing as well, with the possibility of a future charter for nonbank fintech firms as more and more fintechs enter the marketplace. Fact of the matter is, financial brands cannot stave off their demise much longer. Either they follow the lead of the 20 percent of "digital haves" and pursue a bold Digital Growth Strategy, or they get left behind.

Like it or not, it's survival of the fittest out there.

DIGITAL DARWINISM

There's a phenomenon we're seeing where technology, consumer expectations, and the competition are simply evolving faster than a financial brand can adapt or evolve themselves. We call this Digital Darwinism. When this occurs, banks and credit unions get stuck in the **Circle of Chaos** (that we discussed in the introduction).

THE CIRCLE OF **CHAOS**

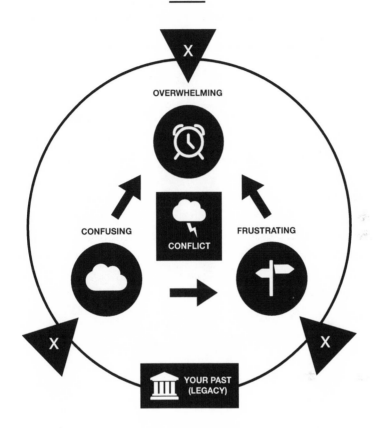

This is how it plays out: first, you have the financial brand leaders—along with their marketing and sales teams—who feel confused by all the changes occurring around them. The confusion leads to frustration when they try new approaches to growth, in marketing and sales, and don't get the result they hoped for.

Well, duh. Of course they don't.

Let's put this in perspective. **Up to this point, financial brand marketing and sales strategic models were built for the physical world of broadcast marketing and psychical branch sales.** Did they really expect to see digital transformation overnight?

Right or wrong, frustration creeps in when marketing and sales teams don't get the results they had hoped for, and that leads to a feeling of overwhelm, as they simply cannot keep up and compete digitally. It becomes a vicious circle. Despite their intentions, marketing and sales teams can't break free from the legacy models and mindsets that have left them completely understaffed and underfunded for digital growth. So the same patterns continue. They end up in a constant state of conflict, just trying to survive and not making any real progress or growth.

> Realistically, you must recognize long-entrenched legacy models and mindsets have created significant structural barriers—to a digital-first growth strategy in marketing and sales—that can't just be immediately overthrown.

When a team is stuck in this Circle of Chaos, one of their very first pain points has to do with a growing technology gap. They fall behind on the marketing and sales technology and become debilitated.

Marketing and sales technology has indeed become the great divider. Again, our research shows 20 percent of financial brands, the digital marketing "haves," are the ones *getting* the technology, the capabilities needed for digital growth, while the other 80 percent are left behind.

To make matters worse, marketing teams are already working at maximum capacity. They are overwhelmed. They and their leadership teams are still trapped in legacy systems, models, and mindsets. They're not letting go of the past.

Moreover, they're not able to keep up with changing consumer expectations, which is the second aspect of Digital Darwinism. As we have learned, consumers are now very much in control of the communication and messaging they receive, through the entire buying journey.

When a financial brand reaches a point where they can't keep up with these ever-growing consumer expectations, it leads to decay, which in practice means erosion of market share.

The same sad outcome is seen when they can't keep up with all the competition coming in. If a financial brand can't fill the consumer need or market gap and their competitor can, *it's curtains* for the legacy bank or credit union.

Digital Darwinism happens when a financial brand can't keep up with all the environmental changes happening around them—whether technology, consumer expectations, or the competition. It all leads to an extinction event, a "retail apocalypse."

A RAY OF LIGHT

Words like "extinction" and "apocalypse" may sound grim and scary, but there's a slight glimmer of hope. Think about the dinosaurs, those once-mighty creatures who ruled the earth. When you take into account the theory of evolution, it wasn't actually the biggest, strongest animals who survived the mass extinctions that took out the dinosaurs but rather the smaller, more agile and nimble creatures who could quickly adapt to the changes in the environment.

Today, digital is like a meteorite that has been cast down on almost every single vertical, including financial services. But as in prehistoric times, it's going to be the more agile and adaptable financial brands who—amid all these environmental changes happening at both the macro and micro level—not only survive but thrive.

What kind of creature are you? What about the rest of your team?

If you believe you have the right temperament to survive the "retail apocalypse," I encourage you to **ask yourself the hard questions**. It's one of the best ways to escape Digital Denial and Digital Darwinism.

In fact, one of my personal maxims keeping me honest is an old Latin phrase, *memento mori*, which means, "remember your death." I bring this up not to be morbid but to encourage you to think of this as the *memento mori* moment for your financial brand, something that keeps you honest with all your thinking and doing. Will your financial brand be here tomorrow? Probably, but what about in the longer term? Will it be here five years from now? How about ten years?

Remember, it was just over a decade ago Steve Jobs changed the world forever when he released the iPhone. Think about that. Ten years is not what it used to be! What roaring disruptions may be coming—coming for you!—over the *next* decade?

No one knows for sure, but we know they're on their way—

and *fast*, because the pace of digital change is exponential. How does that make you feel? Ask yourself the hard questions. Does exponential change excite you? Does it scare you?

> Will your financial brand be here five years from now? How about ten?

One of the most troubling things I hear from financial brand leaders when they confide in me is that they simply don't care about what comes next because they won't be here in five to ten years. They're just coasting toward a path of destruction.

Coasting is deadly: you must find the courage to take a proactive stance and root out the deadwood—cut out the cancer—within your own financial brand.

McKinsey estimates legacy financial brands will see profits decline 20 percent to 60 percent by 2025. How's that for a sobering statistic? PwC (PricewaterhouseCoopers) predicts between 2025 and 2030, we could have a market economy that doesn't include traditional banks at all.

We're talking ten years from now—or less!

Learn from the mistakes of brands in other industries. The CEO of Tower Records used to shrug off concerns about disruption, thinking kids would always want to come to record stores to listen to music! But where is Tower Records today?

Be bold and think *big*. Think in terms of opportunity and thriving not just surviving. Digital is about transforming not just marketing, not just sales, but also your entire growth model—and the choice to commit to this can be one of the most transformative decisions a financial brand leader makes, for themselves, their teams, and their organization as a whole.

COMMITTING TO EMPATHY

In the book's opening pages, we talked about the various Industrial Revolutions and how we're now in the midst of a fourth. What's remarkable about this whole series of revolutions, these massive steps forward in technology, is how they used to come every hundred years or so—but *now* we've cut that in half!

WELCOME TO THE
FOURTH INDUSTRIAL REVOLUTION

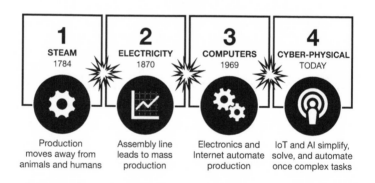

1	2	3	4
STEAM	ELECTRICITY	COMPUTERS	CYBER-PHYSICAL
1784	1870	1969	TODAY
Production moves away from animals and humans	Assembly line leads to mass production	Electronics and Internet automate production	IoT and AI simplify, solve, and automate once complex tasks

It was about a hundred years between the First Industrial Revolution (the steam engine) in the late 1700s and the Second Industrial Revolution (electricity) in the 1870s, and then another hundred years until the Third Industrial Revolution (computers) in the late 1960s and early '70s.

But from there, things started to get really interesting. In the early '90s, we had another huge leap with the internet. And now, really only about fifty years after the rise of computers, we have *cyber-physical*: including the IoT, and AI that is being designed to either—depending on your point of view—(a) take over the world or (b) simplify, solve problems, and automate tasks that were once very complex, to free *us* up for much bigger, better, brighter things.

Clearly, the rate of innovation we're seeing now is extraordinary and a departure from the past. But other elements of these periodic revolutions have stayed the same. For example, if you look back in time, at the macro level, each of these Industrial Revolutions happened during a period of major societal conflict. With the steam revolution, it was our War of Independence. With electricity, our Civil War. The computer revolution was set against the backdrop of the Vietnam War and the tumult of the counterculture.

What about now?

Commentators on all sides of the political spectrum can agree we are living in a time of heightened anxiety and division. Among the concerns in our populace are the existential questions: *What is my place going to be in this cyber-physical future? What is my job going to be? Will I even have a job? Or will a robot take it? And if I don't have a job, how will I make money to pay for my student loans and support my family?*

The point I'm making here is that showing sensitivity to these needs and concerns is essential to doing business in our era. In fact, **empathy** might be the biggest competitive advantage of all in the new digital world.

> In this age of anxiety—over money and more—*empathy* is the most powerful tool in your relationship with your consumer.

If, as we saw in the introduction, these Industrial Revolutions also map out along the same chronology as a series of revolutions in *marketing*—from print to mass media to digital/social media—then the fourth marketing revolution (which we are in now) involves a shift even further toward one-to-one messaging.

WELCOME TO THE
FOURTH MARKETING REVOLUTION

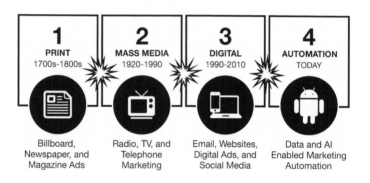

1 PRINT 1700s-1800s	2 MASS MEDIA 1920-1990	3 DIGITAL 1990-2010	4 AUTOMATION TODAY
Billboard, Newspaper, and Magazine Ads	Radio, TV, and Telephone Marketing	Email, Websites, Digital Ads, and Social Media	Data and AI Enabled Marketing Automation

Automation, data, and AI empower marketers to be smarter—with *communication*, once again, at the heart of everything: communication at scale, and at a one-to-one clip. Financial brands who can excel at this, and do it with empathy, will be the winners of tomorrow.

In this new age of marketing, banks and credit unions have to realize they are no longer in control of the buying journey and messaging. **Technology has given rise to an educated and** empowered consumer—*they* control the communication they receive, as well as the individualized buying journeys they choose to take. They do it when *they* want to, not on our account but their account.

This is forcing us, rightfully, to put consumers back at the center of all our thinking and doing. It's not about us. It's not about what we're doing. It's about what people need. When *they* need it. Alex Sion, who is currently leading Citi Ventures D10X program for Global Consumer Banking and was president of the neobank Moven, echoes this sentiment when he says, "Banking will be less about product innovation and more about innovation in the client experience."[2]

Brett King, the founder of neobank Moven, has been very successful doing *exactly that*: innovating the client experience. He once wrote, "Banking is no longer somewhere you go but something you do." But now banking becomes so much more than just something you do, as banking must transform to become something you *experience.*

What do I mean by experience? As it relates to digital growth, an experience is nothing more than a set of systems and processes—centered on the *digital consumer journey*—that have been strategically defined, applied, and optimized over a period resulting in a positive or negative emotion.

From somewhere you go to something you do, to something you experience... financial brand marketing and sales teams can transform legacy growth models.

---

2   Susan Marshall and Torchlite Digital Marketing, "5 Digital Marketing Trends in Banking for 2016," *The Financial Brand*, March 29, 2016, https://thefinancialbrand. com/54885/2016-digital-marketing-trends-in-banking/.

BREAKING FREE FROM THE LEGACY GROWTH MODELS

When we think of the old way of doing business as a financial brand, it's helpful to envision a growth pyramid. Three-fifths (at least) of the pyramid is built around the legacy branch, sales, and broadcast marketing model. Then, when digital came on the scene, digital was bolted onto the pyramid, retrofitted to the old structure.

Are we looking to destroy the old model entirely and start from scratch?

TRANSFORM THE LEGACY
GROWTH MODEL

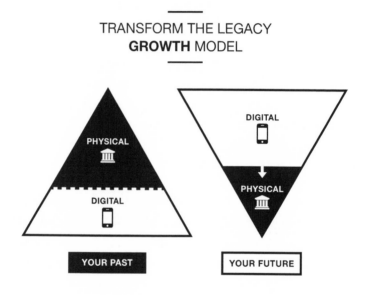

No. Rather, what we're trying to do *is flip the growth pyramid upside down*: transform the entire growth model so it's **now three-fifths digital and two-fifths physical—at a very minimum—as digital becomes the primary driver for growth,** regardless of whether someone applies online, calls into a call center, or comes into a physical branch location to apply for a product.

Digital is at the heart of the consumer buying journey. With the new pyramid, your growth model will reflect that.

In fact, maybe digital might become *four-fifths*—or even 100 percent—of your growth pyramid. I'm not as bullish as Brett King when he wrote the book *Branch Today, Gone Tomorrow*, among others in the same vein. Maybe we'll get to the point one day where the branch is indeed dead. Personally, I'm not ready to say that just yet. People *are* still wanting to come into the branch, just not for the transactions they used to. Now they're coming in for different, specific needs.

From my vantage point, I try to look at everything happening at the intersection of marketing, sales, technology, and human behavior so I can better understand the future of digital growth for financial brands. The way I see it, the future will be built around the following four areas:

1. Communication through the lens of digital and mobile technology platforms.

2. Financial brand marketing teams becoming content and media machines (again, content is at the heart of communication and is going to be the fuel of digital growth).

3. Sales teams transforming themselves, beyond order takers or product pushers, and toward becoming proactive coaches and guides on the consumer buying journey.

4. Using digital channels to become even more empathetic and human—both of which are strategic assets and differentiators in today's digital economy and environment.

Empathy, in particular, is paramount, not just externally but also internally. In transforming and flipping your growth pyramid model upside down, you have to be empathetic to all the people in your organization whose worlds you might be about to literally turn upside down!

There will be a lot of emotion tied to the change. The past growth model was physical, built on the tangible world. You could see it. You could touch it—in branch locations or in the direct mail you sent out. This tactile experience traditionally made us feel good. But the **future is digital**: an intangible world of servers and code. You *can't* see it or touch it. This is understandably a little scary and overwhelming, but now it's the reality of our industry—and our entire world, for that matter.

In the following story, I will show you how this discomfort tends to arise and what it looks like to show empathy when it does.

BRINGING PEOPLE ALONG WITH YOU

A few years ago, I conducted a Digital Growth Diagnostic and delivered a strategic Digital Growth Blueprint for a VP of marketing at a financial brand in Florida. It went great: we showed her what gaps she had and what she needed to do to take the first steps on her Digital Growth Journey.

Up to this point, she had only really dabbled in digital. She had a website, but it was really nothing more than a glorified online brochure. She had placed some digital ads but wasn't sure if they were working because they were being managed through a third party that reported only vanity metrics, clicks and visits, reaches and impressions—not actual conversions. She was also posting some content on social media but wasn't really moving the needle there either.

Following our diagnostic process, we helped her develop a plan and a strategic road map. This gave her clarity, and she felt validated. She took it all back to her executive team, and they started down their Digital Growth Journey. It required a lot of change: it meant stopping some of the traditional marketing they had done up to that point—primarily TV, billboards, and even some newspaper advertising—to create more space and time, and of course budget, to shift into these new digital-first growth initiatives.

The first eight to ten months went smoothly. They built a website that sells and were also starting to run more effective and better targeted digital ads—and creating some exponential value with them, almost out of the gate. Within the first year, digital leads had increased around 1,500 percent. Amazing!

But then something happened.

After about twelve months of making progress along their Digital Growth Journey, the VP of marketing called me and said, "We've got a problem. The board of directors wants to go back to what they were doing before."

"What do you mean?" I asked.

"They're upset," she said. "They're asking, 'Where are our billboards? Where are our newspapers? Why aren't we on TV anymore? Do we just not *exist* in the world?'"

Because the board of directors weren't seeing their brand

and product promotions in the same marketing channels they were used to, they thought marketing had just stopped. It put them in a very uncomfortable and reactive situation. They fell back on old patterns and behaviors that made them feel safe—even though they had seen firsthand over the past twelve months the kind of tangible value digital could create for them when they really committed to it—not just dipping a toe in the water.

The VP of marketing tried to explain this to them, but she wasn't being heard. I could sense her frustration: she had been *trying* to verbalize it all, to share and communicate and educate. But she wasn't breaking through, so she asked me if I could come in and support her.

I readily agreed and flew out to facilitate a strategic training workshop for their board of directors and leadership team that lasted about four hours. It was exactly what was needed. We had a wide-ranging conversation around how people shop and buy in today's digital world and how vastly different that experience is compared to just ten or even five years ago. By helping this group step outside of its specific worldview—as financial board of directors and executives—and into the hearts and minds of *consumers*, they quickly gained clarity about their future growth opportunities just waiting to be captured.

The entire board and executive team quickly connected the dots with their own purchasing behavior: how, for example, when they want to buy something, the first thing they do is run a Google search and read ratings and reviews.

By showing them *empathy*, I disarmed them and they were open to gain new insights. They started to understand **their** marketing team wasn't out to destroy their past built on the physical world of TV, radio, and print marketing. Rather, marketing was committed to transform their strategic growth model to make it more applicable for the digital consumer journey of the future.

The meeting with the board of directors and executive team marked a real, renewed recommitment to digital on the part of the Florida-based financial brand. Now that they've been on this journey for over five years, they've become true believers, as they've maximized their digital growth potential. Their digital channel (website) has moved from their lowest-performing asset to the primary driver of growth—outperforming physical branch locations in the number of applications for loans and deposits.

Above all, my visit helped them to embrace the *mindset* of digital growth, and that has made all the difference.

It's the same with you. To make progress on this Digital Growth Journey, it's vital—even more important than any technology—that you **embrace a mindset that allows you to learn from the past to escape the present,** *and leap ahead into the future*.

A MINDSET FOR THE FUTURE

This means looking at the world and specifically at growth with the 10X mindset we talked about in the introduction. It means transforming your entire thinking about marketing, sales, and growth strategies. Unless you make these changes across the board, it's impossible for you and your teams to realize 10X growth.

Maybe you're on board with some of these ideas and insights but you (or your team) currently have only a 2X growth mindset. That's not going to cut it. And I'm not just being a drill sergeant here: the problem with 2X thinking is you'll find your strategies stuck in the immediate present, because you're focusing only on incremental improvement without fundamentally changing your growth model.

2X thinking will not get you out of the present. You'll still be stuck, trapped in patterns informed by past decisions. "But my teams are working twice as long and twice as hard!" you may argue. "I'm spending twice as much on digital ads!" Okay but ask yourself: does the payoff exponentially outweigh the effort and investment?

I know 10X growth might feel daunting at first. You're transforming *everything* from the inside out: systems, processes, technology, positioning, communication, messaging, and the entire sales and marketing strategy. But I can't stress it enough: developing a 10X mindset will become a huge, strategic competitive advantage for you. Like it or not, it's *the only way* in today's economy, where continuous transformation is required to keep pace with the exponential changes happening at both the macro and micro level.

It's not just marketing. Not just sales. Not just operations or IT. The new thinking of 10X has to permeate throughout your entire financial brand.

Again, it's not about the technology. It's about the people. In fact, **the most important transformations required for digital growth must happen, first, within the individual, then at the team level, and finally throughout the orga-**

nization. Because from there, you can truly transform the lives of people within the communities you serve as you guide them beyond their financial stress toward a bigger, better, and brighter future.

> Your 10X growth mindset will be your strategic competitive advantage.

At the end of the day, you have to get comfortable being uncomfortable. Greatness requires it, and the journey you're taking in this book is one transformation from *good to great*. It's a journey of growth, and you get there by challenging yourself with new ideas, insights, and perspectives. Some of these you might not agree with at first. Some might be difficult and hard to accept. Some might make you feel uneasy. That's the whole *point*.

A 10X growth mindset keeps you from getting too comfortable being *comfortable*, because when you get comfortable, that's when you know you have a problem and are in danger. Your thinking, your strategic outlook...all is at risk of getting stuck in the present moment. This is *not* a place you want to be. In today's digital world, with its exponential rate of change, the present moment is where you'll get run over.

How can you avoid that fate? By getting comfortable being uncomfortable.

WHAT COMES NEXT

When I talk with financial brands—their marketing and sales and leadership teams—and ask them how they feel about digital growth, the three most common answers I get is that they're:

- Confused: because "all this digital stuff" is changing so quickly. There are so many things they know they should be doing, but they just don't know where to begin.

- Frustrated: because what they've done so far hasn't worked as well as they had hoped or expected.

- Overwhelmed: because they're already working at maximum capacity and they simply don't have the time to take on or learn anything new.

But when you dig a little deeper, you'll find some surprising insights. Our research tells us 86 percent of financial brands who have gone through our initial Digital Growth Diagnostic Study do *not* have a defined digital growth strategy providing them with the clarity, courage, and commitment they need to confidently move forward and make progress along their **Digital Growth Journey**.

THE DIGITAL **GROWTH** JOURNEY

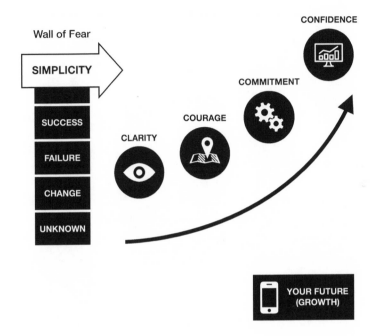

In other words, the answers they give about why they're confused, frustrated, and overwhelmed are, to some degree, a smoke screen for a bigger issue rooted in fear.

But there is hope for all of them and for you. In this book, I walk you through the ins and outs of the strategic tool we call the **Digital Growth Blueprint.** It's a framework to guide you, but I also like to think of it as a strategic marketing manifesto, designed to educate, empower, and elevate marketing and sales teams alongside other key, strategic internal stakeholders.

THE DIGITAL **GROWTH** BLUEPRINT

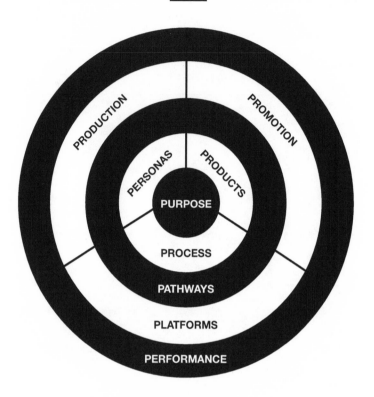

These nine codependent elements include specific systems, technologies, and habits we've developed over almost twenty years of guiding more than 520 financial brands—to help propel them forward into a digital future. It's also based on hundreds of thousands of dollars' worth of primary research we've conducted over the years to put this strategic model into play.

It all begins with a purpose.

Purpose is at the heart and is the foundation of the Digital Growth Blueprint. Do you have a clearly communicated purpose aligning your financial brand with the emotional needs of the people and communities you serve?

That is what we will be discussing in chapter two.

CHAPTER TWO

· · · · ·

WE WILL DEFINE A DIGITAL GROWTH PURPOSE

When Blake Mycoskie was traveling through Argentina in 2006, he noticed a need that got him thinking. In that part of the world, there are a lot of children growing up with no shoes to wear. They're always barefoot.

Not long after that trip, Blake started a company out of his apartment—that company was Toms Shoes (TOMS).

It all began with a *purpose*: TOMS set out to not only sell footwear but to, in their words, also "improve lives." The premise behind their business is that for every pair of shoes sold, they donate a pair to a child in need.

TOMS was one of the founding fathers behind the concept of a purpose-driven brand. In fact, their idea of giving away one item for every item sold is an approach other companies soon followed. It even has its own name, "one for one," which TOMS has trademarked.

What began as a simple idea has now evolved into a powerful

growth model, and the numbers speak for themselves. Since 2006, TOMS has donated more than 88 million pairs of shoes to children.[3] The average price of their shoes is $54, and the average cost of goods (per pair of shoes) is $9.[4]

Clearly, their purpose-driven business model created a triple threat of tremendous value for consumers, kids in need, and the company itself. Purpose gave TOMS a huge strategic competitive advantage in a commoditized shoe market.

But it hasn't been smooth sailing every step of the way for TOMS. Around 2011–2012, their story took a bit of a rocky turn. Truth is, the company lost its way and began to go down a path of conformity.

They became focused on chasing growth and revenue and lost sight of their purpose. To support their expansion efforts, TOMS started to roll out new product lines while moving away from what had made them successful in the first place, falling back on traditional marketing campaigns requiring expensive lifestyle shoots and media placement.

TOMS was no longer focused on the purpose-driven, organic, feel-good, word-of-mouth marketing strategies that were further amplified by social media.

---

3   Kevin Hekmat, "TOMS Founder Blake Mycoskie: The More You Give, the More You Live," Cal Fussman, January 22, 2019, https://www.calfussman.com/podcasts/2019/1/22/blake-mycoskie-the-more-you-give-the-more-you-live.

4   Gennaro Cuofano, "How Does TOMS Shoes Make Money? The One-for-One Business Model Explained," FourWeekMBA, June 8, 2019, https://fourweekmba.com/toms-one-for-one-business-model/.

> A purpose-driven growth model can give you a huge strategic advantage in a commoditized market.

As the company struggled, Blake decided to take a sabbatical to step away and reflect on where he'd been, where he was, and where he needed to go next to transform TOMS. On that trip, he realized the company had become more focused on process and the promotion of commoditized products than on their purpose. They had been concentrating so hard on the *what* of the business and the *how* of growth that they forgot their *why*, their overall purpose—which was still to "improve lives."

Just two simple words: improve lives. But that simple formulation, and the determination behind it, is what had always given TOMS their greatest competitive advantage. It is what allowed them to build an emotional bond with their customers—and for that matter, their employees. It was a motivational factor with both groups. For the people shopping for the shoes and the people working for TOMS alike, *improving lives* made them feel part of something bigger than themselves.

Years later, reflecting on some of these missteps in an article for *Footwear News*, Mycoskie wrote, "We did all the same shit that every other footwear company does. That fucked us up. And that's not what built us in the first place or why people buy our shoes."[5]

Blake stepped away as CEO in 2015, but he stayed on to help drive the company's purpose. He acknowledged that story and

---

5   Katie Abel, "Can Blake Mycoskie's Bold New Social Agenda Reboot Toms?" *Footwear News*, March 27, 2019, https://footwearnews.com/2019/business/retail/ toms-blake-mycoskie-interview-business-sales-mission-1202764082/.

purpose are tightly aligned, sharing the following reflection with *Fast Company*: "I realized the importance of having a story today is what really separates companies. People don't just wear our shoes, they tell our story. That's one of my favorite lessons that I learned early on."[6] Later, during a closing keynote session at the Society for Human Resource Management Annual Conference & Exposition, Blake shared, "**Having a purpose was critical for building a business back then and is even more so today.** When you put giving at the center of a business, something bigger than just making money, your customers become your biggest marketers. They're so proud of supporting your brand that they tell everyone about it."[7]

CHARTING A BOLD AND BRAVE NEW PATH FORWARD IN TODAY'S EVER-CHANGING WORLD

After Blake stepped down as CEO in 2015, TOMS brought in a new CEO, Jim Alling (who had come from Starbucks and T-Mobile). Jim shared with *Footwear News* that TOMS had spent too much time focused on expanding its collection, promoting and pushing the product, and not evolving and growing in the spirit of its original purpose. The way he puts it: "You have to be great at footwear. But **what distinguishes us is our total story.**"

The reality is, it may still be too little too late for TOMS to save themselves. The company may never recover from having fallen away from their purpose.

---

6   Ariel Schwartz, "Toms Shoes CEO Blake Mycoskie on Social Entrepreneurship, Telling Stories, and His New Book," *Fast Company*, October 21, 2011, https://www.fastcompany.com/1678486/toms-shoes-ceo-blake-mycoskie-on-social-entrepreneurship-telling-stories-and-his-new-book.

7   Dori Meinert, "TOMS Founder Blake Mycoskie Encourages Self-Help after Depression Diagnosis," SHRM, August 16, 2019, https://www.shrm.org/resourcesandtools/hr-topics/employee-relations/pages/toms-founder-blake-mycoskie-self-help-depression.aspx.

This is a key lesson for all financial brand marketing, sales, and leadership teams.

In December 2019, Jefferies Financial Group, Nexus Capital Management, and Brookfield Asset Management acquired ownership of TOMS from Mycoskie and private equity firm Bain Capital. The new owners still had faith in the brand and pledged to invest $35 million into the company, money that will, according to CEO Jim Alling, "enable TOMS to further invest in our promising growth areas and continue our commitment to giving."[8]

Moving forward, TOMS's giving strategy will be to donate $1 for every $3 the company makes. Put another way, one-third of net profits will go toward the company's giving fund, and this strategy will allow for more flexibility in its giving, as TOMS engages a new generation of more informed and empowered consumers. According to Amy Smith, TOMS's chief giving officer, this strategic shift ensures the company's purpose will have the greatest impact going forward.

Smith shared, "The consumer is more savvy than ever; they're more engaged than ever; they're voting with their wallets. The combination of TOMS wanting to do as much as we could in a way that was aligned with the passions of our consumers, we really started to wrestle with this idea of: Maybe it's time to evolve a little bit and maybe it's time to do more than just our one-for-one giving."[9]

TOMS's bold move allows them to use data and consumer

---

8   https://www.cnbc.com/2019/12/30/toms-shoes-creditors-to-take-over-the-company.html

9   https://fashionista.com/2019/11/toms-evolves-one-for-one-model

insights to ensure that they are aligned with their consumers in terms of which social issues they focus on and commit to. Toward this end, TOMS also launched the campaign "Pick your style, pick your stand" where shoppers were able to select a specific social issue that the money from their purchases would go to.

There's no denying how hard and scary it can be for a brand to make these kinds of changes to their whole approach and business model. But in the case of TOMS, their boldness and courage may just be exactly what they need to keep moving forward and creating value in the world beyond selling a commoditized product. According to industry news leader *Fashionista*, "A more thoughtful, holistic approach like the one TOMS seems to be going for might be more effective, especially when executed by a company with as much experience with and expertise in giving as TOMS."[10]

Like TOMS, a "data-driven giving strategy" is something a purpose-driven financial brand can implement. For example, consider positioning your checking account around something like "Change for Good" or "Pennies for Positive Change." Every time someone swipes their debit card, your financial brand commits to donating a penny to a local community cause—and also generates revenue from interchange fees. The community cause you support can rotate monthly or quarterly based on the data you gain or collect (through voting contests that further increase organic brand awareness through community partnerships).

---

10 https://fashionista.com/2019/11/toms-evolves-one-for-one-model

FROM SHOES TO SOCKS

TOMS was indeed a pioneer in the world of purpose-driven brands, but they were far from the only ones. This is important, because when I mention them in my talks with financial brand leaders, they often have trouble applying the lessons from TOMS's story to themselves. They doubt the potential for banking on a digital growth purpose to drive exponential growth.

That's when I tell them about another company competing in a commoditized marketplace, Bombas, who has become known as the "TOMS of socks" because of their socially conscious business model (and, of course, because socks and shoes go together). Bombas was founded in 2013, with the *purpose* of supporting the homeless community and bringing awareness to the rampant problem—that the company felt deserved greater attention—of homelessness across the United States.

Like TOMS, for every pair of socks Bombas sells, the company donates a pair to the homeless. Also like TOMS, it isn't just about charity. It's a **business model for growth and profitability that comes from helping other people**, outside of just the key stakeholders of a company.

One of the co-founders of Bombas is a fellow named David Heath. Back in 2011, he came across a Facebook post about how socks were the most requested clothing item at homeless shelters. Again, like with Blake and the origin story of TOMS, Bombas was born out of a genuine impulse to solve a societal problem.

In David's case, after his co-founder Randy Goldberg came on board, the two quit their day jobs and launched on Indiegogo, crowdfunding the whole enterprise. Originally, they set a goal to raise $15,000 in thirty days. But then, to their amazement and delight, they hit $25,000 within just the first twenty-four hours. By the time the campaign was over, they had crowdfunded more than $140,000. From there, they went on to raise another million dollars with seed funding.[11]

Finally, what really helped them take off was landing a deal with Daymond John on *Shark Tank*. It propelled their growth, and within two months of being on the show, they did $1.2 million in sales, selling out all of their inventory.

I use this example of Bombas when I talk to financial executives to show them TOMS isn't a one-off fluke but to also make a case for the **profitability of purpose-driven brands, especially when competing in commoditized markets like almost every financial brand is today.**

> Profitability is what business leaders really want to know about. And profit can be deeply rooted in a purpose that transcends dollars and cents.

How profitable is Bombas? Well, the socks aren't cheap. A twelve-pack of women's ankle socks costs around $145, while a single pair of men's socks is $12. Like TOMS Shoes, these socks aren't for everyone, but (also like TOMS) their story demonstrates how a commoditized product can create a triple threat of tremendous value for multiple stakeholders (consumers, homeless in need, and the company itself). *Major* value: in 2018, Bombas ended the year with $102 million in revenue.

---

11   "Daymond John-Backed Sock Start-Up Bombas Is Bringing in...," accessed December 7, 2019, https://www.cnbc.com/2019/04/16/daymond-john-backed-sock-start-up-bombas-is-bringing-in-millions.html.

Who would have thought the lowly, unglamorous *sock*—the bottom of the totem pole when it comes to clothing and accessories—could be transformed as a purpose-driven brand into a $100+ million powerhouse.

What's next for Bombas? They are continuing to fulfill their purpose as they journey down the path of putting others first. In fact, they've now moved into the T-shirt space, and for every shirt sold, they donate one to someone in need. As of summer 2019, they had donated over 18 million pairs of sock and T-shirts.

Clearly, **purpose is powerful and even more so for commoditized products**; this is true whether your product is socks, shoes, or financial services. In fact, there's mounting evidence, as we'll see later in this chapter, purpose-driven brands continuously outperform traditional ones. This is true both from a financial standpoint—i.e., on the bottom line—and in terms of creating the exponential triple threat of tremendous value for all key stakeholders.

More to the point, if purpose-driven companies are not only competing but also crushing the competition in a commoditized marketplace with their commoditized products like socks and shoes, for goodness' sake, so too can financial brands like yours!

Unfortunately, the vast majority of financial brands are *not* purpose driven.

Instead, they're driven and guided by their traditional mission or vision statements.

A MISSION OR VISION IS *NOT* THE SAME AS A PURPOSE

What is a mission statement, and how is it different than a vision statement? The former is really about us, the financial brand, what we do and how we do it. The latter is also about us in that it provides insight into where we're going as an organization. As we'll see in this section, however, even *that* kind of direction, through a vision statement, is inadequate and not the same thing as what, in this chapter, I am calling upon financial brands to do: define their digital growth purpose.

I'll explain why. But let's start by laying out the four problems, as I see it, with mission and vision statements:

- First, they're *dated*: typically, mission and vision statements were conceived through an increasingly obsolete lens of operating in a physical or tangible environment built around branches and broadcast. But, as we know, the future is *intangible*. The future is *digital*.

- Second, mission and vision statements are bland and *commoditized*: they tend to all look and sound the same. We repeatedly see this through our Digital Growth Diagnostic Assessments. Seriously, you could take a client's mission and vision statement and just copy and paste them to another financial brand. No one would be the wiser!

- Third, mission and vision statements are *self-serving*: they're inward focused and address only the needs of the financial brand. In rare cases where they *do* have some form of external focus, or perspective on the marketplace and customer, it's all very clinical. There's no emotion tied to it. Or it's just very generic and lofty ideas without any concrete substance.

- Finally, and most important, missions and vision statements are *narcissistic*; sadly, that's a reflection of our society as a whole. These mission and vision statements are almost always all about *us*—what *our* needs as a financial brand are.

Redefining mission and vision statements can sometimes feel like you're rocking the boat, and I get why. Often, there's a lot of emotion and history tied up in them. Everyone has an opinion.

This is why there is an opportunity for a "third way" that's not a mission statement, not a vision statement, but something new, different, and truly transformative.

We call this the **purpose statement.**

Notably, the purpose statement is outward-focused and establishes your financial brand's purpose in relation to *others*: the people in the communities you serve. A purpose statement is intended to build trust and create value for people, resulting in a positive emotional response, just like we saw with TOMS and Bombas.

Does this mean you have to toss your mission and/or vision statement altogether? No, but you should place a higher priority on your new purpose statement. Purpose becomes the North Star for your financial brand, the guiding light for where you can go in the future, and a kind of litmus test for decision making.

> Your purpose statement will become your North Star.

Why does it matter so much that your purpose statement, this third way, is not inward-looking like the mission and vision statements?

Because it's that very narcissism and tunnel vision that created the situation we're in as an industry to begin with! It's the reason that people don't trust financial brands. Consumers, for the most part, see financial brands being driven by only their own interests. In fact, a report from Facebook found that 53 percent of millennials feel they have no one to trust for guidance. Even worse, only 8 percent of millennials feel they can trust financial institutions for guidance.

Another study, from Viacom, shared that 73 percent of millennials say they would be more excited about a financial offering from Google, Amazon, Apple, or PayPal than from a traditional bank.

Clearly, money is complex and causing stress for people. But it's not all about the economy. Why are young people trusting Big Tech more than they trust us? It's not just because those companies happen to be the ones they interact with on a daily basis more than any others. Sure, that may be part of it (and one could argue those tech brands are running all of our lives!). But a lot has to do with how we, as financial brands, act, show up, and communicate with the world.

Jack Welch summed it all up nicely when he noted, "Pursuing shareholder strategy or pursuing shareholder value as a strategy was the dumbest idea ever."

WHAT DRIVES FINANCIAL BRANDS AND CONSUMERS

At the C-suite level, financial brand leaders are driven by the **Three Ps: products, process, and profits**. This means the products they bring to market, and the processes and efficiencies they use to reduce costs, which ultimately also drive their profits.

On the flip side, consumers are driven by something totally different: health, wealth, and happiness.

THE DIGITAL EXPERIENCE (DX) GAP

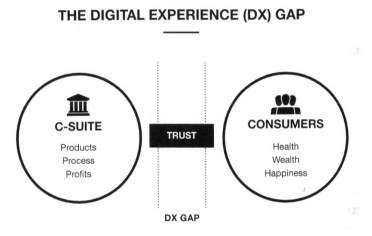

Clearly, those two sets of drivers—the financial brand's and the consumer's—are not fully aligned, so conflict is bound to arise. We call this the Digital Experience Gap, and it can only be bridged by trust. That's why it's in the best interest of financial brands to win over both the hearts and minds of consumers to get more of their business. This creates a certain cognitive dissonance. I know whenever I talk to financial brand leaders about "touchy-feely" stuff like empathy, what they're really interested in is "how does it all affect my bottom line?"

That's an appropriate question, sure.

However, one of the greatest opportunities I see for financial brands to capture is clear: positioning around a purpose that transcends the promotion of commoditized products can generate revenue. Put simply, purpose is the path toward bigger profits. In fact, a growing number of leaders, including some guiding very big brands like Costco, Trader's Joe, REI, and Whole Foods, are championing what they call conscious capitalism—building companies based on the idea their business is about more than just making a profit.

According to *Entrepreneur* magazine, conscious capitalism-inspired companies are outperforming the market by a factor of 10½ and are even beating "Good to Great" companies (classified as such based on Jim Collins's book of the same name) like Fannie Mae and Walgreens by 300 percent.

"Capitalism" is quite a polarizing word in today's political environment, as many feel capitalism is about creating and maximizing profit at the expense of others, creating winners and losers.

But **in today's digital economy, I believe there's an opportunity to transform a mindset of scarcity into a mindset of abundance by reframing and redefining capitalism beyond a zero-sum game.** I like what the conscious capitalism crowd is all about, and their message is very well aligned with the subject of this chapter: defining your purpose as the heart of your digital growth strategy.

All of which is to say, if some of the biggest business leaders today are thinking about capitalism in the context of *purpose* and having a greater impact on the world at large, maybe financial brand leaders are also not driven by the Three Ps as rigidly as it seems.

Furthermore, on the consumer side, maybe the drivers of their behavior aren't as touchy-feely as they seem either.

There's an important difference, though: when consumers brought up *wealth* in their answers to those questions, they didn't necessarily mean being a bazillionaire. People just don't want to feel stressed about money (a lot more to come on that idea in the following chapter about consumer personas). Why? Simple: because this stress takes a direct toll on their health and well-being (happiness).

This is exactly where the opportunity lies for financial brands with purpose. Consumers are looking for someone they can trust to guide them to a bigger, better, and brighter future.

And right now, the neobanks and neolenders are the financial brands positioning around a purpose bigger than profits to bridge the ever-widening consumer trust gap.

What about you? How are *you* going to bridge the consumer trust gap?

PURPOSE-DRIVEN COMMUNICATION AND ACTION

In any human relationship, there are three different levels of connection. In the Pyramid of Human Relationships, the foundation of any relationship, first and foremost, is built on respect, as you commit to placing the needs of others in front of your own. You help someone when they have a need, not when you have a need.

PYRAMID **HUMAN** RELATIONSHIPS

LOVE
I'm ready to
commit to you.

TRUST
Built on communication and actions.

RESPECT
Help me when I have a need. Not when you have a need.

At the pinnacle of the Pyramid of Human Relationships is **love**.

Now, the word "love" might be a bit confusing here at first glance, but there are many different kinds of love. In fact, the ancient Greeks talked about five different levels of love. For our purposes here, perhaps it's easier to think about love within the Pyramid of Human Relationships as *commitment.* Commitment is the deepest form of connection within any relationship between humans. For us, the strategic question to consider is clear: How can your financial brand gain commitment and connection with consumers in the communities you serve in today's digital economy?

The only way to bridge the gap between respect and love is to increase the level of trust. You build trust two ways: (a) communication (what you say) and (b) action (what you do).

In today's digital economy, **trust has to be built with a digital-first mindset**. That's because trust must be established long before a consumer comes into a branch (if they come into a branch at all) to apply for a loan or open an account.

Having a purpose that transcends profits (and the promotion of commoditized products) is your key to bridge the consumer trust gap through your digital communications and actions that are deeply rooted in empathy.

PURPOSE AND EMPATHY

We've already established in today's digital world that empathy is one of the most important strategic competitive advantages, if not *the* most important. But what exactly is empathy?

Google defines empathy as "the ability to understand and share the feelings of another."

To help us better understand the strategic advantage of empathy, let's take a peek inside two brains: that of the banker and that of the consumer.

The beautiful banker's brain tends to be more analytical and rational, as financial brand leaders are often left-brain thinkers relying heavily on fact and reason. This is probably a very good thing for someone dealing with people's money!

However, it is easy for the banker's brain to get trapped in "banker thinking" and view the world only through the three Ps of product, process, and profits. This is why I encourage financial brand leaders to often step outside of their banker's brain and take a stroll into the hearts and minds of people by putting on their consumer caps. When we view the world from the mind's eye of consumers, we are viewing the world through right-brain thinking, driven primarily by feelings and emotions. **Because consumers often buy with the heart— their feelings and emotions—they are always in search of two key things on their buying journeys: help and hope**. How do these needs show up in the brain?

MARKETING TO THE BRAIN

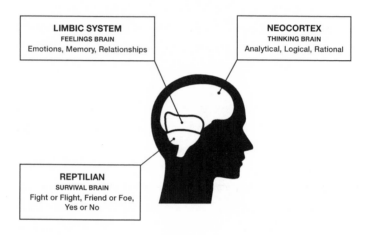

Let's dive a bit deeper into the brain as we explore three key parts together. There's the neocortex, which is the "thinking brain," where logic and reason reside. Then there is the limbic system, which is the "feelings brain," where emotion lives and memories are stored. Finally, there is the "reptilian brain," which is what we depend on for survival.

From a banking perspective, when you find your marketing messages are communicating to consumers about your financial brand's great rates, amazing service, and commoditized laundry lists of look-alike product features, you're very much speaking to their *neocortex* or "thinking brain."

The problem? *Every* financial brand is communicating into a crowded and overloaded "thinking brain."

The opportunity for you is to step back, transform your marketing and sales communication strategies, and speak into the *other* two parts of the brain first.

Here's why: you would create exponential value, for yourself and your financial brand, as well as the people in the communities you serve! How does that sound?

But you can't gain direct access to consumers' limbic systems, their "feelings brain," without first communicating to their reptilian brain. This is where all of your marketing communication strategies must begin.

Keep in mind this part of the brain—the "survival brain"—is all about fight or flight, friend or foe. (You're reading a book about digital, so we'll call it the binary brain: one or zero, true or false, yes or no!) When it comes to consumers, you have to start communicating to the "survival brain" because it's the part of the brain that decides whether it can trust your financial brand.

As such, this is where purpose comes into play in a big way. **When you, as a financial brand, are driven by a higher purpose that transcends the promotion of your commoditized products, you will make an emotional connection in the brain of your consumer.** Their inner reptile is less likely to shout "foe" and more likely to instinctively label you as "friend."

All in all, there's more of a potential for your consumer to trust you—because you're thinking beyond what *you* need as a financial brand and expressing yourself—through your communication and actions, in a way that shows you're attuned to what *they* need.

So far so good. Now you can unlock and access the limbic system, the "feelings brain," which is where empathy is triggered, relationships are formed, and both memories and experiences are stored.

MARKETING TO THE BRAIN

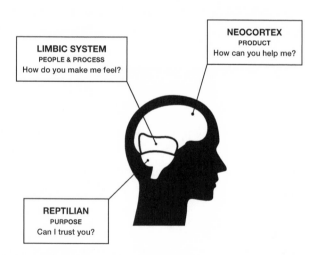

If the primary question the reptilian brain asks is, "Can I trust you?," the question being asked by the consumer's limbic system is, "How do you make me feel?" Similarly, if the first question was unlocked by drawing upon your **purpose**, the question of how you make the consumer *feel* will be answered by how well you leverage your understanding of the emotional needs of **people** within the communities you serve and the **process** (your communication and actions) through which you emotionally connect with them.

If you succeed in making this emotional connection, it means you have empathetically connected to activate positive feelings and emotions through your processes (the communications and actions of your marketing and sales teams).

When you make a positive emotional connection with a consumer, you finally have permission from them to communicate to the rational part of their brain, the neocortex—where it's now okay to talk about your **product**. But even so, be careful to not revert and fall back on old behaviors and begin to babble on about rates, services, and features. Remember, it's still not about you; it's about them. What are *their* needs, and how can you help them?

Through purpose and empathy—enhanced by the communication and actions of your marketing and sales teams—you build respect and trust. That will then activate positive emotions, leading the consumer to fall in love and commit to your financial brand.

What exactly is the value in that emotional connection and commitment? In their report *Making the Emotional Connection of Financial Services*, Motista shared research that concluded an emotionally connected account holder creates 30 percent to 100 percent more value for a brand than even just a "highly satisfied" account holder.

They also identified what is called an emotional multiplier, meaning the value added to an account holder when they analyzed variables such as the number of financial products each consumer held with the bank, whether they considered it their primary bank, and so forth, what Motista found was an exciting multiplying effect: **emotionally connected account holders, established through purpose and empathy, resulted in a 6X multiplier of lifetime value.**

If a 6X multiplier of lifetime value doesn't settle the question once and for all how these strategic principals rooted around purpose, empathy, and emotion are not just touchy-feely subjects and that they create real bottom-line value, I don't know what will!

Thankfully, *you* get it. Now that you know how to use purpose and empathy to win consumer trust through the communication and actions of your marketing and sales teams, you will become better and better at doing it, especially as you learn more about psychology and understand what drives people.

THE FIVE DRIVERS OF HUMAN BEHAVIOR

There are five primary drivers of human behavior, as noted by Harvard Business School professors Paul Lawrence and Nitin Nohria along with Josh Kaufman. First, you have the drive to **acquire**. It's everything you strive to gain: money, status, power. Then there is the drive to **bond**. What you get out of that is acceptance, love, and shared value. Next comes the drive to **learn**. Through education, you gain knowledge, which results in greater confidence. Similarly, the drive to **defend** gives you protection and security. Finally, the drive to **feel** makes you happy and helps you appreciate the beauty of life.

One of the main reasons purpose is the heart of the Digital Growth Blueprint is that purpose binds together so many of these drivers of human behavior, such as the drive to bond and the drive to feel.

And while up to this point we have looked at purpose with a focus on consumers, purpose can also create value internally by aligning key stakeholders across your entire financial brand.

Purpose motivates both internal and external key stakeholders.

Key insights shared by BrightHouse and BCG, as shown in the matrix below, illustrate how motivators of internal key stakeholders can be rational or emotional (and anywhere in between). Motivators can also be anywhere on the spectrum of extrinsic to intrinsic.

PURPOSE **MOTIVATES** PEOPLE

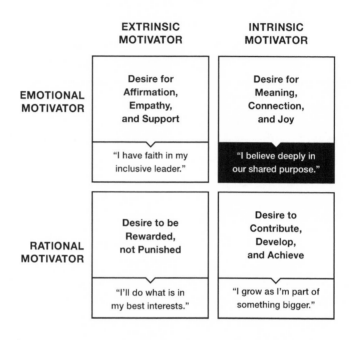

	EXTRINSIC MOTIVATOR	**INTRINSIC MOTIVATOR**
EMOTIONAL MOTIVATOR	Desire for Affirmation, Empathy, and Support	Desire for Meaning, Connection, and Joy
	"I have faith in my inclusive leader."	"I believe deeply in our shared purpose."
RATIONAL MOTIVATOR	Desire to be Rewarded, not Punished	Desire to Contribute, Develop, and Achieve
	"I'll do what is in my best interests."	"I grow as I'm part of something bigger."

Through BCG's research, and looking specifically at gaining internal buy-in for transformative initiatives like maximizing digital growth, BCG found that "purpose is one of the most powerful intrinsic motivators because it speaks to both the head (as the compass that guides and aligns behaviors) and the heart."

Purpose can power your financial brand internally through any massive transformation as BCG shares, "The shift in employees' expectations, together with the demands of always-on transformation, has further exposed the shortcomings of attempting to influence people through carrots and sticks. In far too many transformation programs, people are treated as a means to an end or, worse, as collateral damage."

Furthermore, this kind of purpose-driven thinking can also be applied not only to internal key stakeholders but external key stakeholders as well—consumers within the communities you serve. After all, the anxiety around exponential change, with people feeling overwhelmed, frustrated, and so forth is happening not just within our industry but across all markets as well.

Therefore, the path to your *purpose, the heart of your Digital Growth Blueprint,* must first involve defining it internally with key stakeholders (staff, team members) to emotionally connect with people in the communities your financial brand serves.

This can be an intense, emotional discussion or conversation. But it's worth it, because once you define what your purpose is, you can *communicate* it by putting that purpose in the form of a narrative.

This is how it works.

COMMUNICATING AND APPLYING YOUR PURPOSE

Start by crafting a purpose statement that allows you to communicate your purpose with clarity and simplicity. Your purpose statement will be composed of the following four elements that tie back to the different parts of the brain we just unpacked: there's your *who* (the **people** you're creating value for), your *what* (the value you create with your **product**), your *how* (how you create value through your **process**), and finally, your *why* (the reason you exist—how you want to make people feel—your **purpose**).

PURPOSE STATEMENT PYRAMID

Your purpose (mission) is not about you.
Your moral authority is to help other people.

PURPOSE —————— This is what people buy
Why do you exist:
Can I really trust you?

PEOPLE
Who will you help: Have you
helped others like me?

PROCESS
How will you help: How do you make me feel?

PRODUCT
What value will you provide: How can you help me?

For further context, let's use Digital Growth Institute's purpose statement as an example.

We simplify digital marketing and sales strategies that empower financial brands to generate 10X more loans and deposits (the *what*: **product**). We do this through the Digital Growth Method (the *how*: **process**) that provides clarity for financial brand marketing, sales, and leadership teams (the *who*: **people**) as they gain the systems, technologies, and habits they need to maximize their digital growth potential. As a result, leadership teams no longer feel confused and frustrated about future growth as our research and insights elevate their marketing and sales teams to confidently guide 10X more people in the communities they serve beyond financial stress towards a bigger, better, and brighter future (the *why*: **purpose**).

Once you've defined your purpose statement, it's time to *apply* your purpose, which starts with your whole organization and culture living and communicating it internally. Then you apply your purpose externally in the communities you serve through the communication and actions of your marketing and sales teams. It's what you say, it's what you do, and it's how you build trust with people. Your **purpose statement also becomes a digital positioning statement to attract like minds, both internally and externally, who believe in your bigger purpose** beyond the promotion of commoditized products.

This works not just for the commoditized retail products like shoes and socks. It can absolutely create value for and elevate your bank or credit union. Just look at Aspiration, a purpose-driven financial brand that launched in 2015 and has now raised over $100 million in capital while also acquiring over a million customer accounts. In fact, they've reported adding over 100,000 new accounts every single month.[12]

What is Aspiration's *purpose*? It's twofold: helping people save money and helping to save the planet. They strongly believe they're not just building another commoditized financial company but a community of like-minded people. They didn't set out to be a bank per se. Even on the financial side, they set out with the purpose of building a better world that could put more money in people's pockets and give them more power to do good with their money.

12   Madeline Shi, "A Digital Bank That's Raised over $100 Million Will Pay You to Shop at Do-Good Businesses like Apple and Target," *Business Insider*, February 19, 2019, https://www. businessinsider.com/aspiration-is-launching-spend-and-save-account-2019-2.

They took all of that and distilled it down to four words: "Do well, do good."

That's how Aspiration *communicated* their purpose. But then they had to actually act on their words—and they did, even down to the way they positioned their financial products. One of Aspiration's key product offerings, informed by their purpose, is their pay-what's-fair offer that allows consumers to pay Aspiration whatever fee they believe is a fair amount for their account. This offer was built on their belief that if you want to gain trust, you need to *give* trust. They are so confident that people will love being part of the Aspiration community they're doing what no other financial brand will do when it comes to fees.

> "If you want to gain trust, you have to give trust." —Aspiration

Naturally, there was some skepticism among investors when they launched this strategy. But with their pace of growth, they're proving the skeptics wrong.

Aspiration's primary product is a spend-and-save account offering interest rates one hundred times higher than bigger banks at the time of this writing. They have no ATM fees worldwide. They also have a program that allows their customers to "AIM," which stands for Aspiration Impact Measurement. It means aiming for a better future by tracking your planet impact score based on your spending habits—so you can figure out whether you're spending your money in socially conscious ways. In other words, it helps customers see how their dollars are matching up against their personal values and beliefs.

They're also *acting* on their stated purpose—of helping save the planet—by using only fossil-fuel free accounts. In 2019, there was a lot of bad press around the four biggest global banks—JPMorgan Chase, Wells Fargo, Citi, and Bank of America—for how they were funding fossil fuels. By leaning into the story and positioning themselves against fossil-fuel funding, Aspiration was able to scoop up over 200,000 ex-Wells Fargo customers who left the bank over its recent fossil-fuel debacle, according to CNN.

Aspiration is very clear they're **profit-driven but with a purpose**. Rather than charging those fees to the customer, they're making their money off the spread around the interest rates, along with interchange that is charged to retailers when their customers pay with Aspiration's debit card.

They're also giving 10 percent of every dollar they generate from customers to one of seven charities (chosen by their customers) focusing on helping struggling Americans build a better life. Amazingly, this makes Aspiration the industry leader in giving back, and it allows their customers to decide which social cause they want to focus on.

Aspiration's approach as a purpose-driven financial brand is certainly a bold one, as they also made a public promise that customer deposits would never fund firearms or political campaigns. In doing so, they know they run the risk of alienating certain consumers who are pro-gun or work in fossil fuels, for example.

My intent with highlighting Aspiration here has nothing to do with politics, but I wanted to show **how a financial brand can courageously commit to banking on a purpose bigger than itself**. Aspiration is doing just that, and they're doing very well by it, for both internal and external key stakeholders.

I'm really impressed with what Aspiration is doing, and I'm not the only one. They've gained some attention and investment from big names like Orlando Bloom and Leonardo DiCaprio (in 2019, the latter joined the board of directors when he made an investment as part of series B funding).

All of Aspiration's exciting initiatives are rooted in their purpose, and it's that purpose that propels the brand forward through not only their communications but also real *actions*.

PURPOSE AND PROOF

Without action, purpose is just branding. And for the most part—I hate to say it, but—the branding for most financial brands is bullshit. It's just pretty pictures, colorful logos, shiny happy stock people, not real life.

When it comes to purpose, branding *must transcend* these shallow images. In today's digital economy, purpose *is* the brand. It's why you do what you do.

But the *why* is only skin deep, just like those pretty pictures, if purpose is not backed by proof (the *how*).

PURPOSE **PROPELS** YOUR DIGITAL **BRAND**

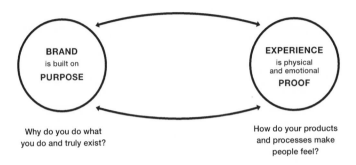

As we've seen in this chapter, defining your digital growth purpose is about transcending the promotion of commoditized dollars and cents. You have an opportunity to position your financial brand around a purpose that educates, empowers, and elevates people as you commit to putting the transformation of people over transactions.

Commit to making purpose your North Star, your guiding light as a financial brand, as you confidently create a path that guides people in the communities you serve beyond their financial stress toward a bigger, better, brighter future.

But remember, your purpose will not be for everyone. Once again, the idea is to define a purpose that attracts those who believe in the value or cause you're bringing to bear through your reason for existence. How do you attract those people? You start by defining consumer personas that represent your ideal account holders. That is the subject of chapter three.

CHAPTER THREE

· · · · ·

WE WILL EMPATHIZE WITH CONSUMER PERSONAS

I was speaking at a conference and sharing insights about the idea of purpose—and about beloved brands who use purpose to bridge the experience gap so well—when someone in the audience mentioned they love Chewy. I'm from Houston, Texas, so my response was, "You mean the Mexican restaurant Chuy's?"

Chuy's is a big brand down here in Texas, with locations in Austin, San Antonio, and Houston. But it turns out the audience member was talking about *Chewy*, the online pet supply company. She just loved everything about her Chewy experience and how it helped her take better care of her pets.

Once again, like all purpose-driven brands, Chewy is not for everyone. It's not for me; I don't have pets yet (just four kids who want a pet so badly). But for this individual, the way the company interacted with her had turned her into a raving fan and regular customer. Fact is, she could probably just go to Amazon and get the same products for less—but she doesn't—

because she appreciates the purpose of Chewy and the value their purpose creates for her (and her pets).

How did Chewy make such a strong impression on her?

Chewy launched in 2011 as the largest "pure-play pet e-tailer" and was bought by retailer PetSmart in 2017 for nearly $3.4 billion. In June 2019, following its IPO, the company was valued at more than $15 billion.

As a purposed-driven brand, Chewy's stated purpose is "to be the most trusted and convenient online destination for pet parents and our partners, like vets and service providers."

They go on to say that "our success is measured by the happiness of people and pets we serve, not simply by the amount of pet supplies we deliver. That's why we continue to think outside the Chewy box, about ways to delight, surprise, and thank our loyal pet lovers."

As you saw in those quotes, not only did Chewy define their purpose as a brand, but they also *tied it to a specific consumer persona*. Again, I am not in that consumer persona, but people who *are* pet lovers and pet parents love Chewy.

Chewy believes the "pet humanization" trend is what is driving an increase in consumer spending on their pets, as 75 percent of pet product buyers in 2018 were willing to pay a premium for healthier pet food products.[13]

---

13   Tomi Kilgore, "Chewy IPO: 5 Things to Know about the 'Pet Humanization' Products Seller," MarketWatch, June 14, 2019, https://www.marketwatch.com/story/chewy-is-going-public-5-things-to-know-about-the-pet-humanization-products-seller-2019-05-03.

Building a business around a niche market consumer persona has positively impacted Chewy's bottom line over the long term. They share, "Our customers spend more on average the longer they remain active, increasing their total spending with us after the first year from their initial order. Customers who remain active on our site spend an average of three to four times as much in their third year as they did in their first year, and total net sales across all customers in that cohort increase over time, reaching approximately 1.5X their first-year sales."

Perhaps there might also be a market to build a financial brand around pet lover consumer personas, too.

CONSUMER PERSONAS FOR FINANCIAL BRANDS

What exactly do we mean when we talk about consumer personas? A consumer persona is just a semi-fictional representation of your ideal account holder, based on market research and real-world data.

Right now, the vast majority of financial brands define their market segments or audiences through demographic data: age, sex, education, occupation, income, and so on. But this isn't good enough. You can't connect emotionally or empathetically with data, something many financial brands, unfortunately, just don't get yet. In fact, in our research, we've found that 68 percent of banks and credit unions have *not* created or defined consumer personas. This is problematic because **without personas, there is no empathy**.

Even among those who *did* report having defined personas, we've learned through our Digital Growth Diagnostic Assessments that the vast majority of these financial brands are not actually *applying* these personas in their digital marketing strategies.

Remember, no personas, no empathy. And no application of personas, no empathy either.

> A consumer persona is a representation of your ideal account holder.

START WITH THE RIGHT QUESTIONS

Whenever I'm working with a financial brand and guiding them through a Digital Growth Diagnostic Assessment, we dive into questions about their ideal audience or market they'd like to attract. I typically get three responses:

- "We want to attract the students," i.e., the 16- to 22-year-olds.

- "We want the prime lenders," i.e., 22- to 40-year-olds.

- "We want the depositors," i.e., 41- to 65-year-olds.

Slight problem here. If they're saying they want *all* these groups, that's basically everyone who's sixteen to sixty-five with money in their pocket and a heartbeat. In other words, they really haven't answered the question! **You can't be all things to all people. If you try to do so, you become nothing to no one, especially with digital marketing.**

This type of thinking—trying to be all things to all people—is rooted in legacy systems, particularly mass marketing. If you go back and look at TV, radio, print, or direct mail, financial brands used to send one message out to everyone in their local marketplace.

Digital, of course, provides the opportunity to segment audiences down into smaller, more well-defined groups, each with specific needs. But financial brand leadership teams still struggle with going down this path. They have a fear of missing out (FOMO): *if we target our digital marketing efforts on this particular group of people, what about everyone else?*

Let me be clear: **digital growth is a result of saying no to "opportunity."** It takes courage to say no and really niche down in identifying specific audience segments you can confidently create value for. This is not an easy exercise—or even an easy conversation to have—but it's one you have to commit to.

In fact, it's really the only way. Why is that?

When it comes down to it, there are three choices, three paths to digital growth as it relates to audience and segmentation. And when we look closer at these three options, we see the only truly viable one is to focus on creating value for a niche. Let's examine:

- You can be a **cost leader** (i.e., a lowest-price option), but this isn't practical for most financial brands because of the high investment it takes to achieve economies of scale. We see cost leadership in the marketplace today with brands like Amazon and Walmart.

- You can take the path of **differentiation** and command a price premium, but this requires extensive research, customized product development, and marketing to a broad segment of people to sustain growth over an extended period. We see differentiation with consumer brands, for example, like Apple and Louis Vuitton, and with high-end luxury auto brands like BMW and Mercedes.

- Last but not least, you can **focus on a niche**, which is where I see the greatest opportunity for financial brands in today's digital economy. Focus limits the competition as you gain the greatest understanding of all of the dynamics and unique consumer needs in a niche market. Once again, perhaps you could be THE most trusted and convenient financial brand for pet parents and partners, like vets and service providers. Or maybe there is an opportunity for you become THE most trusted financial brand for soccer moms in the communities you serve.

Narrowing your focus on a niche market segment doesn't limit your future growth. Instead, it opens up entirely new worlds of opportunities that can only be found through intense focus.

BENEFITS OF THE NARROW NICHE

What else happens when you niche down and focus on creating value for a select group of people?

First and foremost, you create **community**, a concept that has been redefined thanks to digital, as communities are no longer organized strictly around physical boundaries or in-person meeting places. Communities now exist online and are accessible in the palm of our hand. So there's opportunity here to rethink and reinvigorate community in the digital age.

> Financial brands have traditionally been the pillar or backbone of many communities. How can we bring that to the online world?

Another benefit of focusing on the niche is you can finally produce **content** that creates value and helps guide specific groups of people within the community you serve to a bigger, better, and brighter future.

Finally, by focusing on a niche, you limit ad waste and maximize your digital growth potential by getting the most value from limited resources, including money, time, and talent. You focus your content distribution on the relevant **channels** most likely to touch the people in your niche.

All in all, a narrow niche can bring a lot of success and future growth. Just ask REI. Again, consumers can easily go to Amazon and buy camping gear, but instead, they go to REI. Why? It's because of the expertise REI brings to bear around their products for the community they've built through the content they've produced.

Still, it takes courage to focus on a niche. The question you have to ask yourself is: **Are you playing to win, or are you trying not to lose?**

If you're playing to win, you'll be up for the challenge, because you see the value of the narrow niche. You'll realize it's the best path forward for your financial brand in today's commoditized digital world—a world, again, where every other financial brand promotes the same great rates, amazing service, and look-alike laundry lists of product features.

In particular, you'll see how personas bring value to your financial brand by allowing you to humanize the digital experience.

BIG DATA VERSUS THICK DATA: PUT YOURSELF IN YOUR CONSUMERS' SHOES

Empathy is the antithesis of narcissism, and personas allow us to begin to put ourselves in the shoes of our consumers. As the old saying goes, before you can truly understand someone, you must walk a mile in their shoes. That's how empathy is built.

We have to remember that people wake up and say, "I need a car"; they don't say, "I need a car loan." Consumers don't buy your products; they buy *shortcuts to solve their problems*.

So, to begin defining your consumer personas, you have to ask people within your ideal market segment the following:

- What are their questions? What are their concerns? What's keeping them up at night?

- What are their hopes? What are their dreams? What do they want to achieve in the future?

Then the next step is to capture your ideal consumers' data. You do that in two ways.

First, there is the "big data" around these market segments. This data is collected from large data sets, both internal and external, about a group of consumers. In other words, big data informs you about *what people do* by describing consumer behaviors through trends and pattern matching at scale.

But where the real value of persona creation can be found is not in big data but through a term few are familiar with—"thick data." Thick data is the *qualitative information* collected from a subset of individuals to better understand their emotions and the motivations behind their behavior and choices. Thick data doesn't necessarily have as large of a data pool or data set as big data, but the insights gained from thick data can be even more revealing.

BIG DATA VS. **THICK** DATA

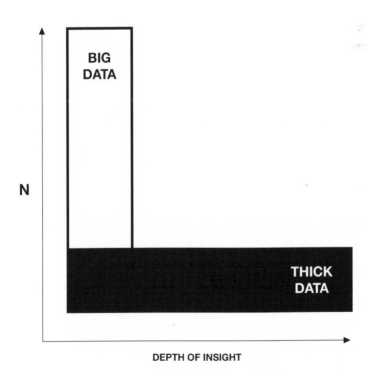

DEPTH OF INSIGHT

Thick data uncovers the why: it provides insight into why people do what they do. To have impact and create value, data needs stories. Without the stories, without the narrative behind the personas, you have no emotional context into why people think the way they do.

It's hard to connect emotionally with demographic data that can look like nothing more than ones and zeros. However, when you put together your personas—utilizing what we call a Consumer Persona Canvas—you get the full picture that peers into the hearts and minds of people. We still need that demographic data, of course. In fact, the consumer persona discovery process actually *starts* with it.

DIGITAL **GROWTH** CONSUMER PERSONA CANVAS

Demographic Data:	
CURRENT REALITY	**BIGGER, BETTER, BRIGHTER FUTURE**
Questions:	Hopes:
Concerns:	Dreams:
Feelings and Emotions:	Feelings and Emotions:
Motivational Makeup: Intrinsic vs. Extrinsic Needs	
Solutions to Cure the Pain:	Channels to Communicate Solution:

Ultimately, though, what we're trying to get at are two sides of the equation gained through thick data: (1) the current emotional reality of your ideal account holder and where they feel stuck by their questions and concerns, and (2) the bigger, better, and brighter future your ideal account holder wants to create by realizing their hopes and dreams.

Together, these insights give us the opportunity to objectively identify solutions that solve the consumer persona's pain along with the channels we can use to communicate the solutions that will guide them to their ideal future.

"Thick data" is the qualitative information collected from a group of individual to better understand their emotions and motivations.

THE FIVE REASONS PERSONAS FAIL

As useful as consumer personas are, they're only helpful and create value when done right. There are five primary reasons personas fail, and it's important to watch out for these red flags when planning and defining personas internally.

1. *Projecting onto the persona*: intrinsically, we believe other people are more like us than they actually are. So it's easy to project our own reality, our own qualities, onto consumer personas.

2. *Describing only buyer demographics*: when it comes to persona development, one of the biggest mistakes I see marketers make is to just profile their buyers' demographic traits, instead of defining their buyer's questions, concerns, hopes, and dreams.

3. *Lacking thick data*: you must go **ALL** in **(Ask, Listen, and Learn)** with personas, whether it be qualitative one-on-one interviews or quantitative surveys or just talking with your frontline salespeople. If you don't have the thick data, you don't have anything.

4. *Developing too many personas*: yes, what we're looking for are common patterns across key market segments, but we also need to keep in mind what resources we actually have as a financial brand to take action with these developed personas and apply them. Pro tip: start by developing two to three key consumer personas.

5. *Relying on focus groups*: focus groups are flawed as they often lead to groupthink. Our Digital Secret Shopping Studies that focus on usability, emotional experience, and lead experience produce far more valuable insights for consumer persona development than focus groups.

I see all of these pitfalls when conducting Digital Growth Diagnostic Assessments. But the one I see the most, perhaps, is number one: financial brands making the mistake of *projecting*.

For example, I was working with a financial brand to develop their first set of consumer personas ever. We started out by taking more of the qualitative approach. We conducted one-on-one interviews, examined the consumers' emotional experience with the brand, and facilitated lead experience testing of their website. Along the way, we documented common questions, concerns, hopes, and dreams. Then we took that data and put it into more of a narrative-like story—a structure that, as we've learned, is much easier to relate to emotionally than the ones and zeros of demographic data. Next, we took those emotive narrative stories and simplified them, distilling them down even further into visual persona graphical elements overplayed with key emotive-driven words.

As I was guiding the marketing team through the consumer persona workshop, the CEO of this financial brand suddenly walked in and asked what we were working on. After we explained to him what the exercise was all about, he stepped back and paused, then folded his arms. You could see he was in deep thought. Finally, he said, "I connect with *that guy* right there" and pointed to an older persona image—one who looked just like him.

What he saw on the white board with this particular persona resonated with him, and he was self-aware that he *wasn't* able to emotionally connect in the same way with some of the younger, millennial personas we had been working on that day.

In this case, the CEO helped the group understand projection because he, unknowingly in that moment, projected himself and his worldview onto a persona. At the same time, the other personas also provided him with perspective into the hearts and minds of *other* people who were not like him, giving the CEO a greater sense of empathy.

From there, this particular financial brand has used the personas we developed together in a variety of amazing ways. For example, they took the personas outside of the marketing department to train their sales teams. Why is this important? We hear from a lot of financial brands how, at the frontline level (both in the branch as well as in the call center), there can be a lack of empathy, especially if the front line doesn't see people like they used to. Personas are a great way to address this challenge and help sales teams become more emotionally connected to the hearts and minds of people they are helping.

This particular institution took it even further and brought the personas all the way up to the board level; so now, when the board of directors is talking about strategy, they actually refer to the names of people in these personas (Josh, Susan, Alicia, Victor, etc.). It helps them to talk about and connect with "real" people, even if the personas are not literally real.

All in all, consumer personas have been very successful in helping this financial brand **drive empathy from the top down**.

You can use and benefit from consumer personas in the same way.

WHAT COMES NEXT

Once you've identified your financial brand's consumer personas—their questions, concerns, hopes, and dreams—you're in a better position to understand how your *products* can serve as solutions and cures to their particular problems and pain points.

There is a great opportunity for you to really lean into their pain points and *lead* with them in your communication strategies. This is important because when we do this, consumers pick up on our visual and written cues: *Wow, they really understand me. They know how I feel. They really get where I'm at today.*

This emotive connection—one that, remember, has to be made digitally—will build trust with your consumers. How do you get there? The only way is to position your products beyond the bullet points, beyond the commoditization of the same look-alike lists of products and features.

This is the subject of the following chapter.

CHAPTER FOUR

· · · · ·

WE WILL POSITION PRODUCTS BEYOND BULLET POINTS

I have an Apple TV remote control, and what amazes me about it and its design is how it's been *simplified*. All the extraneous buttons, if you will, have been removed. It might not be as "flexible" in the sense that the features have intentionally been reduced, but it's easier for me as a consumer to use.

Compare my Apple TV remote to, say, an Xfinity remote, which has a lot more buttons. Sure, there is increased flexibility with the Xfinity remote thanks to more features, but there's also less usability. Put simply, it's just more complex and confusing.

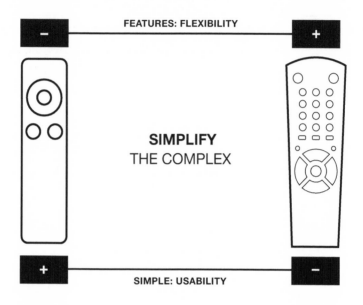

FEATURES: FLEXIBILITY

SIMPLIFY
THE COMPLEX

SIMPLE: USABILITY

When we're talking about financial brands, are consumers looking for features and flexibility, or simplicity and usability?

Knowing money is already an inherently complex subject, **financial brands must commit to removing as much complexity as possible** from the way they position their products and services through their communication strategies.

You have a choice to make here. Do you want to be like The Cheesecake Factory, whose twenty-one-page menu has been called the Bible of Food, with over 250 items? (Some people love that about them, but others find it overwhelming and frustrating.) Or do you want to be more like quick-service chains such as Five Guys, who've simplified their menu down to five or six options, making it more helpful and easier for consumers to decide what to order?

Barry Schwartz has written persuasively about what he calls

the *paradox of choice*. He makes the argument that more choice is actually less. This is because "increased choice decreases satisfaction with matters as trivial as ice cream flavors and as significant as jobs."[14]

> In some cases, too many choices leads to the consumer not making any choice at all.

SIMPLIFY, SIMPLIFY, SIMPLIFY

There is an experience problem with consumers' interactions with financial brands. This problem is rooted in the inherent complexity of money. In our society, we actually don't talk very much about money. It's a taboo subject in a lot of ways. Multiple research studies have found it is easier for couples in a relationship to talk about sex than it is to talk about money.

A lot of this is cultural. Maybe our parents told us we shouldn't talk about it. But it's time for financial brands to remove the taboo because there's a growing epidemic around money, and it's making people sick. Financial stress is literally killing them (stress being one of the leading causes of emergency room visits).

In the research studies we've conducted around digital shopping experiences on financial brand websites, we've asked the question, "How does money make you feel?" More than 1,200 studies later, we've distilled responses down into three negative emotions people tend to have around money:

---

14 Barry Schwartz, "More Isn't Always Better," *Harvard Business Review*, August 1, 2014, https://hbr.org/2006/06/more-isnt-always-better.

- Confusion: "I know money is important, but I don't know what I need to do to keep it, save it, and make more of it."

- Frustration: "I feel like I'm always behind with my money, and there's nothing I can do to catch up."

- Overwhelm: "It just seems like the more in debt I get, the harder it is to get out."

This rise in financial stress has also been verified by third-party research. A study by fintech Stash.com found 62 percent of people find money to be a major source of stress.[15] Another study by Northwestern Mutual also found 85 percent of Americans feel stressed about money.[16]

Clearly, this is something *real*, and it's impacting our physical and mental well-being. The Stash.com study also found 31 percent of consumers are losing sleep over financial stress, and 34 percent feel too embarrassed to talk about it.

Why do they feel embarrassed? This is key: more than a third of survey respondents shared they *think* they're actually worse off than their peers. Meanwhile, 20 percent, or one out of five people, don't talk about money because they are ashamed of their financial habits.

In this kind of environment, **given the level of stress people are feeling, does it make sense, in digitally positioning**

---

15   "Why No One Talks about Money Stress," Stash Learn, October 10, 2019, https://learn.stashinvest. com/money-stress-survey.

16   "Home," Newsroom | Northwestern Mutual, accessed December 8, 2019, https://news. northwesternmutual.com/2016-06-08-Northwestern-Mutual-Study-Reveals-the-Enormous-Toll-that-Financial-Anxiety-is-Taking-on-Peoples-Lives.

your financial products, to prioritize and highlight their complex functionalities?

Do you really want your consumers to have to bear that cognitive load?

THE COGNITIVE LOAD OF MONEY MATTERS

I guided a financial brand through a quantitative and qualitative Digital Secret Shopping Study focused on their website's emotional and lead experience. What we found was a tremendous amount of inherent complexity had been added to the website through the course of its existence.

Their website was about four or five years old. And over time, new pages and content were continuously added without any oversight or due diligence from the perspective of the consumer's digital shopping experience. The website had grown to over 300 different product pages alone! One of our key strategic recommendations was to go through and take a chainsaw to those product pages, chopping away at all that were extraneous and unnecessary. The solution to one of their biggest problems, their underperforming website, boiled down to the **consolidation of content**—bringing everything together in a more unified and simplified view.

Long story short, what this financial brand was able to do is remarkable: with their new, streamlined and simplified website, they increased conversion rates by 1,500 percent. Their marketing team created exponential value because now, unlike before, this financial brand's website had leads streaming in for their sales team to nurture and convert. From a growth standpoint, their website went from their most underperforming acquisition channel (compared to their branches) to outperforming all of their physical branch locations in just eighteen months.

What was their secret? Reducing the cognitive load on their consumers.

Cognitive load simply means the mental energy a task requires for completion. Digitally, we can break cognitive load into three different types:

- There is the **intrinsic cognitive load**, meaning the inherent difficulty of the subject. Obviously, there's already a lot of intrinsic cognitive load built into money and finances.

- But then, there is also the **extraneous cognitive load**, which is the complexity added by how we communicate and present ourselves digitally. This is what we're going to be looking at when it comes to product positioning. As we know, the way financial products have traditionally been positioned is around great rates, amazing service, and look-alike laundry lists of commoditized bullet points.

- Finally, there is the **germane cognitive load**, the schemas or frameworks helping us organize and interpret information quickly—for example, a website's user experience and the frameworks in which information is visually constructed, presented, and communicated.

> There are three kinds of cognitive load: intrinsic, extrinsic, and germane.

Time and time again, our studies have found when a financial brand reduces cognitive load, conversion rates on their website increase exponentially. Similarly, we've seen that with any minor addition of complexity, conversion rates begin to drop.

COGNITIVE LOAD AND CONVERSION RATES

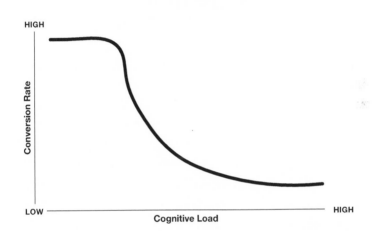

As a financial brand, remind yourself at a big-picture level that what you're doing here is not selling financial products. Again, people don't buy financial products and services; they buy *shortcuts and solutions to solve their problems*. Your financial products are nothing more than a means to an end—to help a consumer reach *their* bigger, better, brighter future.

Now ask yourself, does your website's user experience reflect that basic truth?

Our Digital Secret Shopping Studies and usability studies suggest not.

We have analyzed over 1,200 different digital secret shopping experiences in two ways: on the quantitative side, where we run heat maps, click maps, scroll maps on financial brand websites, and the quantitative side, where we interview people along their consumer buying journey (buying a home or a car, or opening a new checking account, etc.).

One of the most interesting insights from our Digital Secret Shopping Studies is most consumers are not likely to recommend a financial brand website to a friend or colleague looking for a similar banking product, as the overall average Net Promoter Score rating for financial brand website shopping experiences ranks four out of ten.

Our findings are reinforced by a study from Financial Brand that found banking websites actually score the lowest for usability and conversions across all industries. These consumer banking sites also register the lowest perceived *happiness* out of all the financial verticals (compared to, say, a business banking website or personal financial retirement).[17]

What's the solution? How are you going to buck that trend and *differentiate* yourself in today's marketplace where consumers don't think very highly about the digital shopping experiences of financial brands?

I have identified eight specific ways to help you leap ahead and position your products beyond bullet points.

---

17 Jeffry Pilcher, "What Do Consumers Really Want from Banking Websites? Simplicity," *The Financial Brand*, February 13, 2014, https://thefinancialbrand.com/34825/banking-website-design-simplicity-research/.

EIGHT WAYS TO ACHIEVE DIGITAL DIFFERENTIATION

The first way to look at digital differentiation is in terms of **building trust**. Nothing is more important: in fact, the very first question we ask in our Digital Secret Shopping Studies—when conducting emotional experience and lead experience tests on a website—is whether a consumer feels like they can trust the financial brand website we're testing.

As you'll remember from the pyramid of human relationships in chapter two, trust is built upon communication and action.

There are five pillars to establish trust with digital consumers:

- The first pillar of digital trust is simplicity: Have we simplified the complex nature of financial services to provide consumers with clarity? One of the ways you can simplify your website is to transform all those old bullet points and long text paragraphs into headlines and related iconography. The brain processes images 60,000 times faster than it does written text, and 93 percent of all communication is visual. By just changing the way you communicate with consumers on your website, replacing text blocks with pictures and iconography, you begin to simplify their digital experience.

- The second pillar of digital trust is content, the primary way we communicate digitally, which must be focused on helping first and selling second. We'll expand more on this subject in chapter ten.

- The third pillar of digital trust is compassion. Traditionally, we've positioned our products and services through a very narcissistic lens. It's all about us. So again, with digital, empathy—as the antithesis of narcissism—becomes a strategic competitive advantage. (Remember, a primary way we gain and communicate empathy is through the consumer persona strategies detailed in the previous chapter.)

- The fourth pillar of digital trust is connection: people connect with people, not with technology. So when we look at connection, we have to be aware of how we're using people on our website. Do we even have images of people on our website? If we do, are these people shiny, happy stock images who don't represent reality? In our Digital Secret Shopping Studies, we've seen how consumers really pick up on this. They know if the images of people are fake. This is why I'm a big advocate of financial brands taking time to build up a library of photography and images of real people informed by consumer personas. Let people in the communities you serve be the stars, the heroes in the digital narratives and stories you tell.

- Finally, the fifth pillar of digital trust is making the commitment to use digital to guide people toward their bigger, better, brighter future. This isn't dipping your toe in the water with digital; digital has to become your primary growth model going forward. This often requires a culture transformation to break free from legacy thinking and systems rooted around physical branch sales and traditional broadcast marketing channels.

These five different pillars are where we begin to build digital trust in an industry plagued by a lack of it, differentiating ourselves in the process.

The second point of digital differentiation is found through a cultural and organizational commitment to the mantra **"Help first, sell second."** Money is confusing, and people are looking for someone they can trust to help them. This is why helpful content is the fuel of digital growth, and it's what empowers a financial brand to rise above the commoditized promotion of great rates and amazing service.

Committing to produce and promote content that helps first and sells second is very different than the direct marketing financial brands have traditionally relied upon—for example, running a direct product offer around auto loans or running a rate promotion for mortgages.

Helping first and selling second means educating, and in order to do that, you have to build up content assets and content libraries. We'll talk a lot more about that in chapter ten.

The third point of digital differentiation is about **reducing choice**. In one of our studies, we looked at close to a hundred different bank and credit union websites and found the average financial brand website had twenty-eight different calls to action on their home page. That's like twenty-eight different doors a consumer could walk through if they were coming into your physical branch location! Is it any surprise people feel overwhelmed?

HOMEPAGE CTA STUDY

CLICK	CLICK	CLICK	CLICK	CLICK	CLICK	CLICK
CLICK	CLICK	CLICK	CLICK	CLICK	CLICK	CLICK
CLICK	CLICK	CLICK	CLICK	CLICK	CLICK	CLICK
CLICK	CLICK	CLICK	CLICK	CLICK	CLICK	CLICK

NEO-BANK · TRADITIONAL FI

1366 x 768 Screen Resolution

Interestingly, the neobanks and fintechs in this study had only slightly more than six different calls to actions on average on their home pages. Another test we did confirmed that, by reducing choice and eliminating home page promotions, these neobanks also reduced the anxiety of consumers. The Digital Secret Shopping Study testers confirmed they felt like they were being guided, not just promoted or sold to.

The twenty-eight calls to action on traditional financial brand websites are a big problem but not the only problem. There's also the issue of rotating home page banners and promotions. Multiple studies we've conducted have found consumers really don't like these. They think it looks like they're being sold to the moment they hit the home page. Do you blame them?

Furthermore, we've found only about 1 percent of home page visitors click on the rotating banner and promotional ads. Out of those clicks, 84 percent are just on the first banner. Simply put, the rotating banner ad is nothing more than a glorified digital billboard. It's a legacy marketing tactic, a one-to-many messaging tool that needs to be retired for good.

So what do you put on your home page instead of rotating banner and promotional ads? You put your *purpose statement*, the positioning statement designed to emotionally connect with people. This is what you want people to see on their first visit to your website to emotionally connect with them. Then, on their second visit, you can offer personalized guidance as you are informed by the data based on whatever activity they took on their previous visit. For example, if they were looking at mortgages, you can now offer a mortgage buying guide—*not a mortgage buying promotion*—as you help first and sell second.

> Replace your rotating banner and promotional ads on your home page with your purpose statement to emotionally connect with people when they first visit.

That brings us to the fourth point of digital differentiation, which is something we call **guided selling**. Financial institutions no longer have the luxury of talking to someone face-to-face through their buying journey. As much as 70 percent to 80 percent of buying decisions for financial products are now made long before a consumer walks into a physical branch (if they walk into a branch at all) or calls someone in the call center. But that doesn't mean consumers don't want guidance.

As mentioned before, 60 percent of millennials want their bank to be a partner who guides them to a better future. So there are three things to look at here, three questions to think about—through the lens of the consumer—when it comes to guided selling: Where do you want me to go? What do you want me to do? Then, how can you help me get there?

Simply mapping out the steps of what a particular pathway or process looks like for a consumer—the home-buying process, the car-buying process, getting a checking account, getting a credit card—is very helpful and good for using as content blocks on your product pages. We've tested this on multiple websites and have found this simple step-by-step logic makes people feel good because you're telling them exactly where they are, what they can expect, and what they must do next to move forward in their buying journey.

To be clear, this is *very* different than just regurgitating your spiel about product features. Product features are commoditized. Here, you're actually guiding someone through the steps they need to follow.

Moving on to the fifth point of digital differentiation, we come to **product comparison**. Google's "Zero Moment of Truth" study for the financial services vertical found consumers use an average of nine different resources to help them make a decision when getting ready to apply for a financial service product.

In our Digital Secret Shopping Studies, we ask consumers to review product comparison matrices on financial brand websites. Time and time again, we find the visual execution for financial product comparisons often leave consumers feeling confused as they struggle to distinguish different types of products.

What can be done to help improve and optimize the comparison of different products on your financial brand's website? We recommend two major moves: (1) add a guided selling product recommendation quiz that provides a personalized solution based on a consumer's unique situation, and (2) benchmark and position your financial brand's products on your website directly against your competitors' products in the marketplace.

Again, we know consumers are going to comparison shop. They control the entire narrative now. But anchoring your products against your competitors gives you some influence over the narrative.

The sixth point of digital differentiation has to do with **limited time offers**. We have found through our Digital Secret Shopping Studies, and also guiding clients over the years, that whenever we run "flash sales" for a particular product, we get immediate results. Limited time offers really move the needle. It's simple supply and demand: when it comes to product scarcity, limited supply in a virtual shopping environment can increase demand and as a result, drive conversions.

At our son's science fair, he conducted an interesting experiment designed around the idea of product scarcity. He had two cookie jars. One was filled to the top. The other had just a couple of cookies at the very bottom—it looked like it had been pretty much depleted. Then he asked people to come and taste cookies from both jars. After they ate the cookies, he asked which one tasted better to them and found for an overwhelming number of respondents, the cookie in the jar with fewer cookies "tasted better" than the one in the jar filled to the top. Of course, they were exactly the same cookie.

> Limited time offers do move the needle in digital, but limit your use of "flash sales."

Moving on to the seventh point of digital differentiation, we have **social proof**, as the vast majority of consumers say reading reviews is important before making a banking decision. This is why **thinking about consumer reviews and online reputation management as part of the entire consumer journey is so critical—reviews (and even review stars) really do influence people's buying decisions.**

When I talk about reviews here, I'm mostly talking about venues like Facebook and Google Places. But another kind of simple win is to get third-party reviews and validation from other industry websites like GOBankingRates, Kiplinger, and NerdWallet.

The most advanced implementation of social proof is to actually integrate a platform on your financial brand's website to capture Amazon-like reviews where users can click on the number of stars and leave a comment.

Finally, the last point of digital differentiation is **value packaging**, which looks at how we package our product to create exponential value.

Cornerstone Advisors conducted a study and found if Amazon were to bring a checking account to the marketplace and bundled in value adds (e.g., cell phone protection, ID theft protection, and roadside assistance), more consumers would be open to paying a small fee for the account versus an unbundled free checking account. As Ron Shevlin notes, "The real lesson from this data isn't simply consumers' interest in getting a bank account from a non-bank. **It's their willingness to pay a fee for a checking account when there are value-added services bundled with the account.**"[18]

Bundling value is a great way to differentiate product.

We're seeing product bundling play out in the cell phone world now, where phone companies are adding complimentary products as part of their commoditized services. Sprint has the bundle with Hulu, AT&T has one with HBO, T-Mobile with Netflix.

As for financial services, if we know consumers are stressed out about money, and this stress has a negative impact on their physical and mental health, **why not bundle a mobile banking app with a mental wellness or meditation app? Or checking account with financial coaching?**

To that last point, I see bundling up financial coaching, both in person as well as remote, as one of the biggest untapped product differentiation strategies and opportunities in today's digital economy.

For example, let's assume you offer three different levels of coaching: Basic, Standard, and Premium. The Basic coaching option is something all account holders get access to through an online, digital community.

The Standard option is then bundled into your most popular

---

18   Ron Shevlin, "Do Consumers Really Want to Bank with Amazon?" *The Financial Brand*, January 23, 2018, https://thefinancialbrand.com/69921/amazon-bank-checking-account/.

checking account to create even more value for consumers, as it includes a personalized annual financial strategy session plus quarterly coaching calls to keep them on track. You might even charge a nominal fee for this account—say, for example, $9.95 per month. Imagine, for a moment, how this checking account with expert coaching would be positioned against your competition, who is, of course, still just offering commoditized free checking.

Finally, say you charge $99 per month (generating non-interest income) for your Premium coaching option, which includes access to personalized one-on-one coaching calls every month. You can take this thinking even further by offering a guarantee that if your financial brand coaching program does not help a person achieve their goals or does not find ways to help them save at least $1,200 per year, they get their money back. Of course, this would require a commitment on the part of the consumer as well.

In summary, think of these eight digital differentiation tools more as items in your digital toolbox you can pull from to position products beyond bullet points. You don't have to use every single one. If you commit to apply a few on your website, in your emails, and on your digital ads, you will digitally differentiate your financial brand's products and begin to generate even more leads for loans and deposits almost immediately.

WHAT COMES NEXT

Over the past four chapters, you've learned how your financial brand can build a strong foundation for digital growth.

It's a lot to think about, right? I get it. Building a strong foundation is hard work and often requires courage and commitment to make some pretty big decisions that impact not only marketing but the entire organization.

That's why I often find financial brand teams typically want to jump ahead and skip the foundational strategies.

Don't. That's a big mistake.

When teams think they are saving time by jumping ahead, what they're really doing is just staying stuck in the present moment. This misjudgment is typically rooted in a lack of awareness of what's happening in the real world with all the technology-driven changes in consumer behavior and their competition.

But you're not going to make that mistake. *You're* doing this the right way and you will be prepared. By defining your **purpose** as your North Star, you have greater clarity and direction on where you're going to create value for consumers—the people in the communities you serve. That alone—purpose—will create value for you and your financial brand as you align around something more than just your commoditized products and services.

You also understand the importance of **empathy**. You know if you don't take time to create your **personas**, it will be very hard for you to empathize with your consumers' hopes and dreams. But by taking the time to understand their questions and concerns, you can lean into consumer pain points to help encourage and spark changes in behavior through your content as you commit to **help first and sell second**.

Your **products can be the cure to their pain,** but only if you are able to help them see your products as shortcuts to their bigger, better, brighter future.

Finally, you know you have to differentiate your product—beyond the great rates, the amazing service, and the commoditized look-alike lists of bullet features every financial brand promotes—and you are doing that with an understanding of the inherent complexity, stress and anxiety people feel around money.

Now you can look for ways to reduce those anxieties and create value at every step in your consumer's buying journey.

PART TWO

———

BUILD A DIGITAL
GROWTH ENGINE

Now that we've established a foundation for digital growth, we're ready to create even more value. This is where the rubber meets the road and growth actually happens.

It's also where you apply all the thinking you've accumulated so far to continue forward and make progress along your journey of transformation.

In the Digital Growth Engine, we take different components and technologies and put them together, mapped out and aligned around the digital consumer journey, which must remain at the heart of everything we do.

* * * * *

CHAPTER FIVE

WE WILL ESCAPE THE DANGERS OF DOING DIGITAL

Digital pioneers like Amazon have played the long game. In building their businesses for the long term, either they lost money in the early days or broke even. They weren't "profitable" because they were reinvesting back into their business and using those resources to create infrastructures, systems, and processes that would lead to future profits at an exponential scale.

Early on, Jeff Bezos made it clear profit was not his short-term goal. Amazon finally turned a profit in 2003, nine years after being founded and seven years after going public. Furthermore, for additional context, in just the first quarter of 2017 alone, Amazon booked as much profit as it had earned in the first fourteen and a half years following its initial IPO in May 1997.[19] That's huge—and a great example of playing the long game for exponential growth.

---

19 Alison Griswold and Jason Karaian, "It Took Amazon 14 Years to Make as Much in Net Profit as It Did Last Quarter," Quartz, February 2, 2018, https://qz.com/1196256/it-took-amazon-amzn-14-years-to-make-as-much-net-profit-as-it-did-in-the-fourth-quarter-of-2017/.

The problem is, traditional brands have a different mindset.

Take Walmart: losing money to play a longer-term game goes against their nature. They want to make profit quarter over quarter, year over year. But when Walmart first tried to move into the digital space, it seemed like maybe their approach had shifted and they were going to become more like Amazon.

At the time, they paid over $3 billion for Jet.com and tapped the Jet CEO Mark Lore to lead their digital division and really integrate digital into their store operations. This was no small investment for Walmart. But they knew they had to *go big* to take on Amazon with its two-day shipping, in-store pickup kiosks, curbside for grocery, and so forth.

Reports have come out recently forecasting Walmart's e-commerce division is predicted to lose $1 billion in 2019 alone on sales of $21–$22 billion.[20] Frustration seems to be brewing within the company, with leadership looking to make changes. Under current CEO Mark Lore, there's more scrutiny of the digital division even though Walmart as a whole is in a more competitive position than it was before it acquired Jet.

How it all turns out is an open question. Walmart knows that to succeed in digital will require not just modifying how they operate digitally but how they operate in the physical world as well. To compete with the e-comm leader, to play the same game as Amazon, means Walmart may continue to lose money in the short term as they transform their physical

---

20 Jason Del Rey, "Inside the Conflict at Walmart That's Threatening Its High-Stakes Race with Amazon," Vox, July 3, 2019, https://www.vox.com/recode/2019/7/3/18716431/walmart-jet-marc-lore-modcloth-amazon-ecommerce-losses-online-sales.

locations to also serve as digital fulfillment centers capable of competing with Amazon's new one-day shipping offer.

The biggest challenge Lore must overcome is a slew of traditional retail leadership mindsets refusing to invest in the future because they abhor operating losses that cut into short-term profits. But unfortunately, it is those short-term gains that ultimately come at the expense of longer-term growth.

Is this a battle Lore can win? Possibly, but my guess is it's already too late.

Time will tell. But regardless, digital simply cannot be bolted onto a traditional growth model built for the physical world.

A PROACTIVE APPROACH TO MARKETING

As we saw in the example of Walmart, it's not easy to break free from the legacy mindset of TTWWADI (That's the Way We've Always Done It). It means letting go of the idea that future growth will come from the physical world. In the case of financial brands, that means branch sales and broadcast marketing.

According to a study from Adobe, marketers feel like marketing has changed more in the last two years than in the last fifty years.[21] One of our own Digital Growth Studies found 77 percent of financial institutions feel like they lack digital marketing capability and/or capacity, meaning they're having a hard time keeping up with those changes. The challenges

---

21   Gbaconqz, "Marketing Has Changed More in the Past Two Years than in the Past 50," Quartz, August 18, 2015, https://qz.com/132776/marketing-has-changed-more-in-the-past-two-years-than-in-the-past-50/.

are obvious—and evidenced by an article by *Harvard Business Review* that puts fuel on the fire, claiming marketing departments are still operating like it's 1990 or even earlier.[22]

> Financial brand marketers are confused, frustrated, and overwhelmed.

What's at the heart of this issue? The challenges for financial brand marketing and sales teams are not as much about technology, or lack thereof, as they are about structure and the way we think about and view the world around us.

In particular, the majority of financial brand marketing and sales teams have operated for far too long from a **reactive** stance. We wait for people to come to us and say, "I need help with this," or, "I need a loan," or, "I need a checking account."

In today's digital world, we can—and have an obligation to—take a more **proactive** stance in the lives of the consumers we're committed to helping, to make recommendations and offer coaching and guidance, long before they raise their hand.

This is where I see a tremendous opportunity to do away with legacy marketing and sales department structures that operate as independent entities. Because marketing and sales are often siloed, they are driven by two very different perspectives and goals. Instead of thinking about marketing and sales as independent activities, begin to think of them as one and the same.

---

22 Mei Lee, "Too Many Marketing Teams Are Stuck in the Past," *Harvard Business Review*, August 19, 2016, https://hbr.org/2014/09/too-many-marketing-teams-are-stuck-in-the-past.

Marketing supports sales. And sales supports marketing. But that's not always the case, as I often hear from marketing teams that sales is not doing their job following up with leads. I also hear sales teams complain that marketing is not getting them leads—or the right types of leads—to follow up with.

MARKETING & SALES BECOME THE **GROWTH** TEAM

It is for this reason I recommend combining marketing and sales teams to create the Growth Team—headed up by the chief growth officer—where marketing's primary goal, in addition to generating leads for loans and deposits, is to control and manage the financial brand's message and experience through communication and action. Sales can then pick up those leads, with a primary goal of nurturing and then converting and closing those leads for loans and deposits. Marketing and sales can then both hold each other accountable with a "Lead Management" service level agreement as they work together toward unified goals.

I learned the power of being proactive in marketing and sales early on. I was the second round of hires at Old Navy when

Old Navy first came to the Houston market, and we actually became the number one-selling Old Navy in the entire country! Our success was all attributable to our incredible training. It was so simple. Whenever someone entered the store (even though this was a brick-and-mortar retail store in 1999, the lessons learned are still applicable today in digital), we should say hello, walk them around the store, and basically shop *with* them. Guide them. Help them. We took a very proactive stance in terms of the shopping experience, and because of our success, we even started doing training for all the other Old Navy stores opening in the Houston market.

The same thing can happen digitally. We must take a proactive stance and reach out with a helping hand. It is time to stop being reactive and simply waiting for someone to walk through the proverbial digital door (consumers aren't doing that anymore!).

A proactive stance means going beyond just dabbling in digital, and it means more than just taking old legacy methodologies and cramming them into the new digital space. This is a problem I see all the time: taking the strategies and systems of broadcast marketing and trying to shove them into, for example, the website (with the rotating banner ad). Or taking the old idea of a direct mail blast to everyone within a three-mile radius of your branch and shoving it into a nonpersonalized email that goes out to every single account holder regardless of their need.

There are a lot of legacy methodologies still finding their way into digital. Instead of these one-to-many messages, what financial brands *should* be focusing on are one-to-one messages based on where each consumer is in *their* buying journey.

Communication patterns and marketing messages should change depending on whether someone has just started their journey or are closer toward conversion and purchase. Messages should also change based on the persona type.

Again, I get it: it's hard to shift the way we operate and think. We all know we have to change, but knowing and acting on it are two very different things. Change is scary. Here's the thing, though: if it were easy, everyone would be doing it, right? When it comes to digital growth, the desire to change has to be greater than the desire to remain the same. It's that simple. Otherwise, nothing's going to happen, and we end up getting stuck in the present.

Remember, in the introduction I talked about the **Four Fears: people are scared of the unknown, they're scared of change, they're scared of failure, and they're scared of success**. Until you overcome these four fears *yourself*, you will not achieve 10X growth.

THE FOUR TRANSFORMATIONS FOR
DIGITAL **GROWTH**

That's why there are four transformations that must happen to maximize your financial brand's digital growth potential, and it all starts with the self—with you. Only then can you move from the individual to transform the team and expand out to transform the entire organization. Finally, with marketing and sales aligned around a higher purpose, you can transform the lives of people within the communities you serve as you guide them beyond their financial stress toward a bigger, better, and brighter future. I've seen this time and time again: not everyone is going to be on for this ride. And that's okay. You can't change someone's mind. But you *can* start to *transform* mindsets.

In fact, let's stop talking about "change." Let's remove the word from our vocabulary because, again, change is a very scary idea. But on the other hand, the journey of *transformation* leads to something even greater for everyone involved.

> Don't change minds; transform them.

DEVELOPING THE DIGITAL GROWTH MINDSET

Mindset is more important than technology on the journey toward exponential digital growth. It's even more important than the asset size of a financial brand.

There are two very distinct types of mindsets I see in financial brand marketing, sales, and leadership teams.

The first is the **legacy mindset,** which looks at the world and says gloomily, "My best days are behind me." The legacy mindset gets stuck dwelling in the past. As for digital, people with legacy mindsets tell themselves they're never going to make it in this brave new world because they "just don't have the capabilities" they need. Of course, this is a self-fulfilling prophecy and a way of avoiding the challenges—challenges they must, in the end, commit to taking with courage and confidence. Instead, they're scared of facing any type of criticism or of failing, so they give up. They quit.

The second type of mindset I see is the **growth mindset,** which looks at the world and says with gleaming eyes, "Our best days have yet to come; our best days are ahead of us." People with growth mindsets are excited and energized about the future.

Whenever I have a Digital Growth Diagnostic Assessment call, it's clear to me within five minutes how the person on the other line views the world—and it's usually predictive of the success both they and their financial brand will have over the next twelve to twenty-four months. Financial brands with the greatest success are the ones who approach digital with a growth mindset.

A person or brand with a growth mindset is always looking to learn and gain new insights that exponentially expand their capabilities. People, teams, and organizations with growth mindsets are excited about solving big and important problems. They welcome criticism and look at failure as an opportunity to learn.

How can *you* develop a Digital Growth Mindset? There are twelve key traits to focus on. I liken it to running a marathon, as you'll see in each of the following stages:

- *Assessment*: When you run a marathon, you don't just start running. You go to the doctor for a health check. An assessment can also create value for you, your team, and your organization when embarking on your Digital Growth Journey.

- *Awareness*: This comes from training and planning. Again, if you're running a marathon, you don't just start running 26.2 miles on day one. You have to train your body and follow a plan that guides you. The same is true for you and your team, as training and planning helps you become aware of the roadblocks you must eliminate and the opportunities for you to capture as you make progress and move forward along your Digital Growth Journey.

- *Acceptance*: This is where I see a lot of financial brands struggle. They assess their situation and have awareness of what they need to do next, but then they don't accept the fact—whether as an individual, team, or organization—that some things are going to have to change. They don't accept that they are probably going to have to make some tough decisions. As a result, they fail to fully commit to take their next steps forward on their Digital Growth Journey. When you sign up for a marathon, there's an acceptance on your part: you have now committed to a specific goal to be completed in the future.

- *Adaptability*: When you're training for a marathon, you have to adapt and modify your behavior. Change your diet, change your lifestyle, get up in the morning and put the miles on even when you don't want to. When you are committed to moving forward and making progress along your Digital Growth Journey, you will also have to adapt and modify behavior—as an individual, as a team, and as an organization—as you build new systems, processes, and habits.

- *Attitude*: When you're training for a marathon, things are going to get tough and probably not go as you expected or planned. That's why 90 percent of marathon running is mind over matter. The same is true when you're moving forward and making progress along your Digital Growth Journey. Keeping and having a positive attitude for yourself, for your team, and for your organization is crucial and is what's going to help you get through the tough times. If you don't have a positive attitude, you're going to fall back on old behaviors, patterns, and habits, ending up exactly where you were when you first started.

- *Abundance*: Training and running a marathon creates a tremendous opportunity to come together with others—not compete against them but run *with* them. In life as well as with digital growth, we must choose to view the world as either abundant or scarce. When we choose abundance, we see unlimited opportunity and the potential to collaborate with others to create value—even "competitors" like fintech or other financial brands. The opposite of abundance is scarcity. That's where we find ourselves always worried there will never be enough resources (time, money, and talent). As a result, we turn inward and begin to view those around us—even our closest coworkers and peers—as competitors or, worse, enemies.

- *Action*: Race day has arrived. You've trained up. You're at the starting line ready to go. This is when shit gets real. You've got 26.2 miles ahead of you. Now is not the time to get scared and back out. It's time to just *go*: take your first steps and start running. No one is going to do this marathon for you. You are. And the same is true for any progress you make on your Digital Growth Journey. You must commit to take action and move forward every single day, even if it is just one step at a time. I've seen some of the best plans and strategies for digital growth go to waste because when the time came to take action, move forward, and make progress, the financial brand marketing, sales, or leadership team got cold feet—they had not properly developed their Digital Growth Mindset.

- *Automation*: Technology automates tasks that used to make training for and running a marathon difficult. That's why on race day you're fully prepared and ready to go, as your GPS watch automates tasks that were once very manual (or even impossible) like tracking your heart rate, distance, pace, splits, elevation, calorie burn, and so on. Monitoring all of these can have a positive impact on your finish time. Automation—along with AI—now helps you maximize your digital growth potential, as you become even more efficient by automating predictable and repeatable marketing and sales activities.

- *Analysis*: As you make progress along your run, your GPS watch automatically crunches data from multiple sources (heart rate, distance, pace, etc.). This gives you the ability to quickly analyze your performance with every single step you take. With digital marketing and sales, you must also analyze multiple data points in real time to ensure you maximize your digital growth potential.

- *Adjustment*: When you analyze your running performance in real time, you are also able to make adjustments in real time to ensure you achieve your marathon time goal as you speed up, slow down, and watch your heart rate. Be prepared to do the same as you move forward along your Digital Growth Journey. Don't be afraid to adjust your pace as needed to protect yourself and your team from burnout.

- *Accountability*: When you're running a marathon, you're not running alone. You're either running with a team of training partners, or you're running with hundreds or thousands of others who are all working toward the same goal as you are. You need people alongside you, too, during your Digital Growth Journey—whether someone internally, at another financial brand, or even the Digital Growth Institute—to ensure you don't fall behind or get off track. It is helpful to have these partners to guide you and hold you accountable, helping you move forward.

- *Authenticity*: You're off and running on your marathon. You feel good. Everything is going great. It's a perfect day. Then you hit the dreaded wall between mile 18 to mile 20. This is when the race becomes more mental than physical. This is where you must be true to yourself and remember why you started down this path in the first place. And just like running a marathon, you will hit the wall on your Digital Growth Journey. And when you do, falling back on and staying committed to your financial brand's purpose—your North Star—empowers you to keep pushing forward. It helps you focus on and measure not how far you still have to go but how far you've come.

Of course, to do any of this, to develop your Digital Growth Mindset, you need to give yourself time and space to work on it. You can't always just be doing digital.

THE FOUR OPERATING ENVIRONMENTS OF DIGITAL GROWTH

What I see with financial institutions through our Digital Growth Diagnostic Assessments is the vast majority get stuck *doing* digital. And the only way to get unstuck is, again, to create space and time to work in the other Digital Growth Operating Environments, the first of which is **learning**.

DIGITAL **GROWTH** OPERATING ENVIRONMENTS

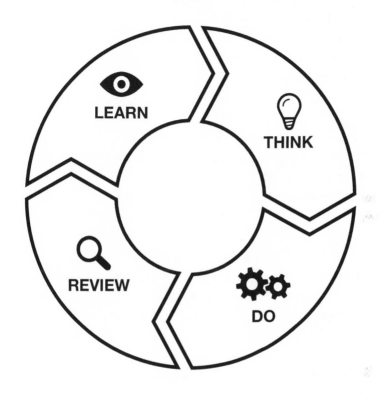

As the world continues to change at an ever faster pace, learning—and the clarity that comes from it—is the antithesis to fear of the unknown. The future doesn't seem so scary when you have an idea of what it looks like and what the opportunities are available for you to capture.

> Learning eliminates the fear of the unknown.

Once you have clarity about the future opportunities for digital growth, you must then apply the insights you have learned. This is where the second operating Digital Growth Operating Environment—**thinking**—comes into play. This thinking domain is where you define strategies and develop systems and processes for future digital growth. When it comes down to it, that's what digital marketing and sales is: systems and processes.

Now you're ready to apply your thinking—your digital marketing strategies, systems, and processes—to your next round: **doing**, which is the third Digital Growth Operating Environment. Here, you'll find your *doing* and implementation of digital marketing strategies have now become even better. Instead of continuing to operate from a reactive stance informed by legacy systems and processes, you've now confidently transformed to a proactive practice of marketing. Here, your actions have been strategically thought out and informed by your newfound digital marketing knowledge and insights.

Finally, in the fourth and last Digital Growth Operating Environment, once again you create space and time to break free from *doing* digital as you **review** and reflect on everything you've just done. Digital growth requires a process of continuous optimization. What value did we create? What's working well? What lessons have we learned?

The goal for you and your team is to cycle through and operate in each one of the Digital Growth Operating Environments every ninety days. This ensures you will never get stuck *doing* digital again.

Traditionally, financial brands go through an annual strategic planning process, but I don't feel that's viable anymore when it comes to marketing, especially considering how fast the world is moving now with digital. We need to shorten the learning curve—and shorten the strategy model to ninety days.

Over the ninety-day period, you will create space and time, guided by the Digital Growth Operating Environments, as you ask: What new insights are we learning and gaining this quarter? How are we applying these insights to develop new strategies, systems, and processes? What must we commit to do next as we apply these new strategies? What value did we create over the last quarter, and what were the greatest lessons we learned?

WHAT THIS CAN DO FOR YOU

To escape *doing* digital—and create space and time to learn, think, and review—is very much a strategic competitive advantage that can transform you, your team, and your financial brand.

There's nothing wrong with *doing* per se. If no one did anything, nothing would ever get done. But the problem with *always* being stuck in *doing* is that doing is really all about the present moment—and the present is informed by those decisions from (and successes of) the past, which as we learned in chapter one, can keep you stuck in the here and now. And that's deadly.

This was very much the case with a particular marketing team we worked with. They came to us extremely frustrated. In fact, they're a perfect example of feeling confused, frustrated, and overwhelmed because they had so much on their plate. Other key stakeholders in their organization would always ambush them at the last minute—"we need to get this out to market!"— and so they got stuck in *doing* marketing. No surprise that as they tried to move toward a path of digital growth, they couldn't gain any traction.

One of the very first things I encouraged them to do was to start saying "no," or at least start saying "not yet" to all the requests coming through. I recommended they use an Agile model for marketing strategy built around ninety-day cycles with three columns of work: To do, Doing, and Done.

This helped take away a lot of the emotion of saying "no" or "not yet." When any requests came in from key stakeholders, they put those requests in their "To do" column and then had an objective conversation about what value the particular task they were being asked to do might create. They also looked at whether they truly had the capability or capacity to do it. If it was an urgent matter, they could tell the person asking for it that yes, they could push it through, but it would mean pausing other activities in their "Doing" column.

Once an approved strategic task got moved into the "Doing" column, there were four action modes it traveled through: (1) Plan, (2) Produce, (3) Promote, (4) Performance. Each action mode was built on the previous one and also informed the next one. This Agile approach to digital growth provided a visual framework of their entire marketing operations and available capacity.

THE DIGITAL **GROWTH** AGILE MARKETING MODEL

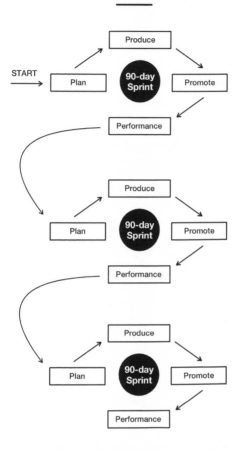

By using these tools, the marketing team started having much better, more objective conversations. Slowly, over time, they completely redefined their role internally. No longer were they there to serve the last-minute needs of others but **rather to be the driving force for future digital growth**.

Funny thing is, they *used to* feel super busy but never productive. Being busy is not being successful. I see a lot of marketers who feel like they're successful because they're always busy. (When you ask someone, "How are you doing?" and they say, "Oh, I'm so busy," they're giving you a bullshit answer to mask deeper operational problems. It's a side note, a separate conversation for another day, but an important point to take a moment to stop, pause, and think about for yourself right now.)

Now, three years later, this financial brand marketing team is in a completely different place and positive state of mind, doing important, meaningful work, not just being busy. Their morale has increased exponentially. It's almost like a different group of people.

By having the courage to say "no" or "not yet," along with the tools and resources to support those difficult conversations, they went from feeling like a glorified in-house FedEx Kinko's to confidently planning the path for their financial brand's future digital growth.

They were also able to transform beyond the traditional seasonal quarterly campaign cycle to operate around ninety-day growth sprints. The digital consumer journey became the heart of their marketing operations model, and now it informs all of their thinking and doing.

By creating space and time to think strategically, they were able to plan marketing strategies around each stage of that digital consumer journey, a subject we'll explore in depth in the following chapter.

CHAPTER SIX

• • • • •

WE WILL MAP OUT DIGITAL CONSUMER JOURNEYS

For our honeymoon, my wife and I had originally wanted to go to Bora Bora. We had been talking about this for the longest time. Bora Bora was our dream but sadly not in our budget back then. What could we do instead? I knew I wanted our honeymoon to be an experience we'd remember forever.

So I got online and Googled. With Bora Bora out of the running, I had no idea where we were going to go, but I started doing a ton of research. I probably researched for a good three months looking for the perfect destination. Finally, with the help of TripAdvisor, I was able to narrow our honeymoon down to three or four locations and properties.

One of these was a little boutique hotel called Ladera on the island of St. Lucia. At the time, 2006, St. Lucia hadn't blown up as a tourist spot like it would in the following years. Obviously, there was tourism there, but the place was still wonderfully quiet and quaint. (Later, the island was featured on *The Bachelor*, which brought travelers in droves!)

The neat thing about this particular hotel, Ladera, which I found through my research and all the positive ratings and reviews, is that it's situated about 1,500 feet above a bay between two extinct volcanoes. The whole place is open and exposed to the environment. There's no AC: you don't need it because you're so high in elevation that you always have a cool breeze running through. Also no phone, no TV, no internet—the perfect place for a honeymoon.

I bring this up to make the point that although I spent a lot of time and energy (digitally) researching the place in advance, once we got there, it was all worth it. I had picked the perfect spot—and I did it all *myself.* I was in control, and I didn't have to go through a travel agent like people used to before the days of digital.

In today's buying journey, the consumer is in control. The way people shop and buy has changed forever. As financial brands, our job is to help facilitate the journey based on the unique situation of each individual consumer.

Pre-internet, the buying journey was so simple: there was point A and point B. First, you had some type of broadcast marketing stimulus—TV, print, radio—and this is what drove the consumer into a branch location. Then they would meet with a financial brand representative, get a loan, open an account, and so on. That was that. Life was good for financial marketing and sales teams.

THE LEGACY **CONSUMER** JOURNEY

Post-internet, the path is more like point A through point Z. There are just so many other way points we have to consider now as a financial brand guiding consumers along their individual buying journeys.

When I was researching a honeymoon hotel, I was anxious about messing things up, especially going to a place I had never been before. This was our honeymoon, after all, a once-in-a-lifetime experience! Consumers shopping for financial products feel that same anxiety or even greater. They want to be sure they're making the right choice. They're looking for help and guidance.

I can't stress this enough: you need to understand where

they're coming from and empathize with what they're feeling, which is why it's so important to **map out their digital consumer journeys**.

But where do you start?

With a piece of paper and a whiteboard. Analog. Ironic, right? It all comes back to creating space and time to step into those other operational areas to *learn* about human behavior, how people are shopping and buying financial products, and then apply that thinking. This isn't about fancy technology. It's about pen and paper and sticky notes.

It's also where the golden opportunity lies for marketing to redefine their role beyond frustrated order taker to strategic leader—to show what marketing digitally is really about.

What *is* it about? Systems and processes. Experiences. Marketing teams have the opportunity to redefine their role as *experience engineers*. And to engineer these experiences, they have to think and plan and map.

Digital consumer journey mapping is one of the most essential strategies that can maximize your financial brand's future digital growth potential.

Sadly, it's still an anomaly in our industry.

WE MUST ADDRESS THESE INDUSTRY PAIN POINTS

From the research we've conducted year over year across the industry, we've found 84 percent of financial brands have not mapped out digital consumer journeys. Why is this such a problem? If you don't have a digital consumer journey mapped out, just think what it means for the person on the other end trying to navigate the complex world of buying a financial product. It's like asking them to walk through the woods at night alone without a flashlight. Sooner or later, someone's going to get hurt!

A study from CUNA Mutual found 61 percent of borrowers shared they felt "anxious, stressed and/or afraid at some point before or during the loan application process."[23] Simply taking the time to map out consumer journeys from a digital-first perspective will absolutely help reduce the anxiety people are feeling when they're shopping and applying for a financial product.

Unfortunately, not only have most financial brands failed to do this, but they're also losing business around their consumer application process, which is another huge pain point. Our year-over-year industry studies have found 83 percent of banks and credit unions do *not* have what we call an abandoned application process—meaning, when someone starts an application but abandons it, there's no way to even know who the person was, let alone follow up with them. Just think of all the lost opportunity!

> When you haven't mapped out your digital consumer journeys, it's like you're asking consumers to walk through the woods alone at night without a flashlight!

---

23   Steve Heusuk, "Create Loyalty and a Better Experience with a Strategy You Might Not Expect," CU Management, August 9, 2019, https://www.cumanagement.com/connect/skybox/2019/08/05/create-loyalty-and-better-experience-strategy-you-might-not-expect.

The more you can understand how people actually shop for and buy financial products in today's digital economy, the better position you're in to address problems like abandoned applications and bridge these gaps.

So how *do* people shop and buy? From our research, we have found 87 percent of bank shopping journeys start online. How do we know this? When we conduct Digital Secret Shopping Studies that include lead experience and emotional experience testing of financial brand websites, we actually ask people how they would go through the shopping process. Most (87%) say, "We'd start with Google." The other 13 percent say, "We would ask a friend or talk to friends or ask on social media and *then* go to Google." (In other words, the number is really closer to 100 percent!)

When it comes to other financial products like mortgages, there have been studies like Ellie Mae's, which found 92 percent of people who bought a home within the previous year did their research online before—and this part is key—reaching out to a lender.[24] Similarly, a study from Jornaya found that 60 percent of mortgage customers visit more than one third-party website before shopping for a loan.[25]

It is also important to understand just **how *long* the buying journey is these days for people in the market for financial products**. For a deposit product, like a checking account, we're talking two to three months on average from the time

---

24 "Digital Mortgage Solutions Improve the Loan Process, New Ellie Mae Survey Finds," Ellie Mae, accessed December 8, 2019, https://www.elliemae.com/about/news-reports/press-releases/digital-mortgage-solutions-improve-the-loan-process-new-ellie-mae-survey-finds.

25 "A Mortgage Consumer's Journey Can Provide Steady Insight in a Fluctuating Market," Jornaya, May 29, 2019, https://www.jornaya.com/a_mortgage_consumers_journey-0/.

someone starts looking to when they actually convert. But for mortgages, that window can be six months or even longer!

What are consumers doing during that six-month period? They're looking for help!

Earlier, I mentioned an important report from Google Insights, the "Zero Moment of Truth" study conducted through the lens of financial services. Another major insight that came from this study is consumers use an average of nine different sources of information to help them make a buying decision, and 57 percent comparison-shop bank products online, just like I did when I was comparing properties for my honeymoon.

Ultimately, what Google found, and what we have found through our own Digital Growth Secret Shopping Studies, is **human interaction—even if it's just a two-minute interaction online via email, chat, or even video—is still the most influential source in a consumer's buying journey for a financial product.**

Human interaction doesn't have to be face-to-face, but it must be all about the *experience*.

THE EXPERIENCE FORMULA FOR GROWTH

Earlier in the book, I expanded on the idea from Brett King (whose thinking has influenced me a lot) that banking isn't just somewhere you go but something you *do*. I suggest banking must also become something you *experience*.

Once again, we've defined experience as nothing more than a set of systems and processes—centered on the digital consumer journey—that have been defined, applied, and optimized over a set period resulting in a positive or a negative emotion.

Now we're taking this idea of experience and connecting it with digital consumer journey mapping, through the formula **DX + HX = Growth**.

DX is the digital experience, and HX is the human experience. As we will see, growth is not about one or the other. It can only happen when the two work hand in hand together.

Let's walk through this equation piece by piece, starting with the **digital experience**, which is actually made up of three sub-experiences. First, you have your lead experience (LX), then your customer experience (CX), and finally your referral experience (RX). The digital experience (DX) is the sum of all three multiplied by the emotional experience (EX) delivered digitally.

$$DX = [LX + CX + RX][EX]$$

Just like digital experience (DX), the human experience (HX) is also made up of two key sub-experiences, as people are seeking two things central to their own human experience: Help (He) and Hope (Hp). One important note: when it comes to their financial situation, people do in fact seek hope before help, as they truly long to escape the current financial situation they feel trapped in. Finally, both help and hope are further amplified when empathy (Em) enters the equation through empathetic communication and messaging strategies.

HX = (He + Hp)(Em)

When mapping out digital consumer journeys, we need to consider all of these different experiences as we take into account
the five consumer needs that are directly related to the stages
of the buying journey.

THE DIGITAL **GROWTH** CONSUMER JOURNEY

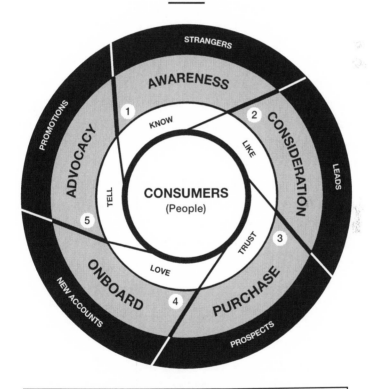

THE FIVE CONSUMER NEEDS

FIVE STAGES OF THE CONSUMER JOURNEY

FIVE TYPES OF CONSUMER RELATIONSHIPS

Stage one is the **awareness** stage: that's when a consumer is a stranger and needs to get to know you first. Stage two is the **consideration** stage: when a stranger becomes a lead and begins to like you and what you stand for (your purpose). Stage three is the **purchase** stage: when a lead becomes a prospect and has gotten to the point of trusting you enough to apply for a loan or open an account. Stage four is the **onboarding** stage: when a prospect becomes an account holder because they "love" you and you "love" them—that is, commitment. (This love is tied to onboarding because it's where the consumer wants to be affirmed in their buying decision.) Finally, stage five is the **advocacy** stage: when an account holder loves you so much they want to tell the world how great you are.

To recap, we have awareness (knowing), consideration (liking), purchase (trusting), onboarding (loving), and advocacy (telling). These are the five stages of the buying journey directly aligned with the five consumer needs.

Some of you may already be familiar with these ideas, but I've found it's very helpful for financial brands to have it all together in a framework like this and to be able to see digital experience as a whole through this lens of the consumer's buying journey.

> The five stages of the digital consumer journey are awareness, consideration, purchase, onboarding, and advocacy.

Expanding further on this thinking, we developed an operating methodology aligned to these journeys called the **BANCER** (pronounced "banker") Strategy Circle. This is an acronym to help you remember six key strategic actions that align marketing, sales, and service activities around a centralized operation methodology.

The **B** stands for *building* an audience to increase website traffic. The **A** is *attracting* qualified marketing leads with personalized offers. The **N** is *nurturing* sales qualified leads with automation and content to increase trust. **C** means *converting* sales qualified prospects into new loans and deposits. **E** is *expanding* relationships by delighting account holders through onboarding. And **R** is *repeating* this process with ratings, reviews, and referrals.

BANCER'S STRATEGY CIRCLE FOR
EXPONENTIAL DIGITAL **GROWTH**

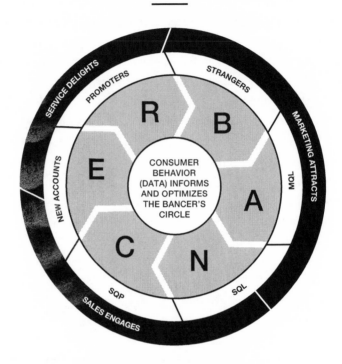

1. **BUILD** an Audience to Increase Website Traffic
2. **ATTRACT** MQL with Personalized Offers
3. **NURTURE** SQL with Automation and Content
4. **CONVERT** SQP for Loans and Deposits
5. **EXPAND** Relationships by Delighting Accounts
6. **REPEAT** with Ratings, Reviews, and Referrals

Let's look at how this plays out in practice.

THE CONSUMER JOURNEY OF BUYING A HOUSE

We worked with one financial brand to define a digital growth journey for a particular mortgage product offering of theirs, which was featured on their website. All they had really focused on before was the conversion stage of their consumer's home-buying journey—the call to action, if you will. We recommended they also focus on the consideration stage, on consumers who showed some interest and intent in buying a home but maybe weren't ready to apply just yet.

A primary strategy for the consideration stage included the production of a key piece of content called *The Complete Guide to Buying the Home You Love*. This was a meaty document, about forty pages, and they not only put it on their product page for download as a transitional call to action for those not ready to apply for a mortgage, but they also gave the guide its own landing page to run targeted ads against. It is here, in the awareness stage of the buying journey, that we recommended placing ads not for the mortgage product itself but for the buying guide. This positions the financial brand as a helpful guide.

All in all, based on intent data we had, we helped the financial brand *build their audiences* to target. Then we served up an offer to that audience and *attracted marketing qualified leads* with the home-buying guide on the landing page. Next, we *nurtured sales qualified leads with automation and content* related to the home-buying process. And finally, we *converted sales qualified prospects* by getting people to apply for a mortgage or schedule face-to-face meetings with a mortgage advisor, again putting human beings in touch with other human beings.

Your digital consumer journeys must always put people at the center of all of your thinking and doing.

Even as we've seen 87 percent of consumers starting their

buying journeys online for financial products, interestingly, however, we're also seeing the **in-person, in-branch experience have the highest pull-through and conversion rate for digital leads**. It's a paradox: digital is still driving in-branch leads. But why? In part, it has to do with the problem I mentioned earlier with the application abandonment process, as 85 percent to 92 percent of online applications are abandoned.

From an e-commerce standpoint, that's like someone leaving something in their shopping cart and not clicking the Buy button. There's intent there, but then something, some friction (most likely frustration in the application itself), causes the person to abandon the app and jump ship. Obviously, if we don't know who those consumers are, we're losing the opportunity to get them to come back and complete the application process.

> Eighty-five to 90 percent of online applications with financial brands are abandoned by the consumer before they are submitted.

There may be a digital paradox at play for now, but the central fact remains that consumer journeys are completely different than they used to be: they're much longer, and the majority of journeys start *online* with consumers comparison shopping and very much in control of the entire buying experience *themselves*.

Mapping out digital consumer journeys is a strategic priority for financial brands in today's digital world.

The financial brand in the story I just told was able to transform themselves beyond legacy thinking by doing exactly that, by looking at their mortgage experience through the lens of the digital consumer buying journey and then making sure they had the right systems, processes, content, and channels in place to move someone from one stage to the next.

You can do this, too. In fact, you should apply and repeat this exercise for every single one of your product lines guided by the BANCER Strategy Circle. But remember, it's an ongoing process. Once you apply the first iteration, come back again, review, and learn from what worked and what didn't. Then optimize to make it even better the next time around.

Because automation plays such a key role in the digital consumer journey, we have to ensure you have the proper *technology* platforms to empower both your marketing and sales teams, the subject of the following chapter.

When it comes down to it, technology is just the medium for bringing two human beings together. Your digital consumer journeys will be built on the back of technology. And even though digital consumer journeys may be at the heart of your digital growth strategy, without technology, your digital journeys would never become reality.

CHAPTER SEVEN

WE WILL MAXIMIZE MARKETING TECHNOLOGIES

It's very hard to believe in this day and age, but **the company that invented the digital camera was, in fact, Kodak.** They did this all the way back in 1975. From a quality standpoint, this first digital camera definitely wasn't there yet: it took pictures that were only 10,000 pixels, which would be 0.01 megapixels in today's terminology. But they *had the technology* and they didn't stop there. They kept investing in digital, patenting different innovations along the way. In fact, many of the camera technologies we use today were created back then by Kodak.

So what happened? Later on, at the moment when it really counted, Kodak ended up putting their digital camera concepts on the back burner. They continued to build their business around the physical and tangible world of film.

Despite the fact that in 1995 they *did* actually bring their digital camera to market—and were even a market leader at the time (because they did it before so many others got in the digital game)—their dominance didn't last long. They didn't take advantage of their early entry into the marketplace.

They were stuck in the present moment, making strategic decisions informed by their past. They weren't planning for future growth.

Kodak's growth was far too dependent on the legacy model of film and printing, all rooted in the physical, intangible world. Why did they never embrace and go all in on digital (especially given they had the technology before anyone else)? Here's the crux: if they had done that, it would have meant cannibalizing their own business.

Therefore, there was never really an incentive for them to continue to invest in the future. If they *had* done so, it would have come out as a "cost." Does that sound familiar? It's the same conundrum we talked about with Walmart in chapter five.

> Kodak was deterred from going all in on digital [technology *they* created] because they weren't willing to cannibalize their existing business.

Netflix had a similar choice to make. They started out in the physical world with direct-mail DVD delivery but crucially avoided getting stuck in the present and making decisions based on their past success. Instead, they disrupted and transformed their entire business model, literally putting everything at risk to invest in the technology of streaming media. Now they continue to reinvest, building on their success with streaming, as they've essentially become a production company.

By going all in and investing in the technology, Netflix transformed their business model—not once but twice! That took courage and commitment. Kodak, on the other hand, had the technology from the beginning but failed to invest in maximizing its potential.

What lesson can we take from these contrasting stories?

Above all, it's this: **what got us to where we are today *won't* get us to where we need to be tomorrow.**

What that means for financial brands is that branch sales and broadcast marketing will not get us far in a new world built on the intangibles of digital marketing and sales strategy.

SIMPLIFY MARKETING TECHNOLOGY

There's an annual report called the *Marketing Technology Landscape* that looks at all the different marketing technologies available, broken down and categorized by element. According to the latest report, there are now over 7,000 different marketing technologies available.

It wasn't always like this. The first *Marketing Technology Landscape* report, back in 2011, showed only 150 marketing technologies. Since that time, we've seen a 4,500 percent increase in marketing technology options! What's behind this explosion? Traditionally, when we talk about technology for financial brands, it's all been through the lens of online banking, mobile apps, lending platforms, and so forth. But things have changed. Technologies are no longer just for IT or account holder services (online and mobile banking). Now, going forward, we must look at **technology as a growth**

and acquisition opportunity, driven by marketing and sales teams.

In fact, it was predicted (by Gartner) that chief marketing officers (CMOs) will outspend their IT counterparts (CIOs) on technology.[26] This shift is already creating some internal friction and power struggles within organizations. Again, I welcome the shift (of technology becoming a marketing and sales priority and not just an IT thing), *but* financial marketing and sales teams need to think about technology the right way.

With 7,000 options, it's easy to get confused and mistaken about what they really *need*. Don't let this be you. Don't just get swept up by the latest hype. What I see happen a lot is that a financial marketing, sales, or leadership team member will go to a conference and hear about a new technology that's supposed to be a "game changer." But in reality, it's all just rainbows and unicorns—especially when it comes to CRM (a big pain for a lot of financial brands) as it sounds great in theory, but in practice and application, there's still a huge gap.

Everyone wants the coolest, latest thing. I call this "digitoolitis," or bright shiny object syndrome. What they're missing is that none of these tools are going save them. It's like me going down to Home Depot, buying a shovel, a saw, some board, and hammer and nails and trying to build my own fence. Without a plan, my fence is going to look horrible. It's the same thing with financial brands: technologies are useless without a strategic framework and some critical thinking about how it all fits into the bigger picture.

---

26 Nadia Cameron, "Gartner: How CMOs Will Spend More on Technology than CIOs in 2017," CMO Australia, accessed December 8, 2019, https://www.cmo.com.au/article/612861/gartner-how-cmos-will-spend-more-technology-than-cios-2017/.

That's why the implementation and rollout of these tools typically don't deliver with what the tech platforms are promising. The teams using them often don't have a well-defined strategy.

> Digitoolitis = a common condition of addiction to shiny marketing and sales technologies without an understanding of how they fit into the bigger strategic picture.

Again, **technology is nothing more than a tool to bring two human beings together**.

Here we are, halfway through the book, and we're only *now* talking about technology. That's intentional. Yes, technology is important, but only if we're using it right. To do that, we have to simplify what's complex.

Escaping the complexity of technology with a simple path is exactly what our Digital Growth Engine is designed to do.

BUILD A DIGITAL **GROWTH** ENGINE

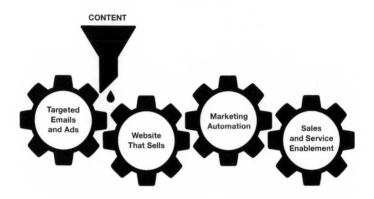

The Digital Growth Engine has four gears, representing the four types of technology platforms needed for exponential digital growth, and they are also aligned with the consumer buying journey.

Let's go through them one by one.

THE FOUR GEARS OF THE DIGITAL GROWTH ENGINE

The first gear is **targeted emails and targeted ads**. The goal of this gear is to increase website traffic.

The second gear is a **website that sells**. The goal of this gear is to generate leads from that traffic being driven to the website.

The third gear is a **marketing automation platform,** utilized to capture and nurture those leads being driven to the website.

Finally, the fourth gear is **sales and service enablement**, which is designed to convert those leads into loans and deposits and expand those relationships and opportunities.

Those are the four gears of the Digital Growth Engine. But like any engine (car engine, airplane engine), you need something to power it, a fuel source.

The fuel source of the Digital Growth Engine is *content*.

Content is the fuel that powers and turns each of the four gears and that moves someone from one stage of the buying journey to the next. Remember, we can't just think of technology in and of itself. We have to look at in the context of the digital consumer journey.

Furthermore, we have to think about technology in terms of what *kind of content* we need to power it in a way that maximizes the fuel.

That's where data and analytics come into play, and it all happens on the **dashboard**. The role of the dashboard in the Digital Growth Engine is to take raw data and turn it into analytics that you can actually interpret. Then, once you interpret the data beyond ones and zeros, you can gain insights.

Think of this like the dashboard of a plane. When the plane is ascending, the dashboard shows how much altitude you're gaining. It provides direction and tells you if you need to course-correct.

That's the Digital Growth Engine in a nutshell: four gears, with content as the fuel, and the dashboard telling you where you need to go. These are the important elements you need to understand. It's not about this or that specific technology but rather the overall strategic model.

Look, I get questions all the time, for example, about what marketing automation platform I recommend. I can't answer that for you in this book. Platforms can change, and it depends on your unique situation and capabilities. Do you need an enterprise solution? Or would an SMB solution be ideal? Do you have the capacity, the talent, and staffing needed to maximize these technologies? What about an objective strategic road map to guide you along the way? Again, I've seen some really bad rollouts of marketing and sales technologies across the board—like six-figure marketing automation deals go south.

Technology companies love to sell you their platform, and they make it look so easy. But then in practice, the financial brand that buys the technology—for example, a marketing automation solution—and doesn't have the necessary content to power the platform. Honestly, in this example, the financial brand could have gotten the same value from a $100/month subscription to an online form builder instead of wasting

$100,000! I've also seen struggles when financial brand marketing and sales teams don't have the full organizational and cultural buy-in to really make good use of these technology platforms. In fact, I see this often on the marketing automation and CRM side.

Again, what matters most is the Digital Growth Engine and its four gears. Content is the fuel. But there is also another element I think of as the *oil* that helps the four gears to run smoothly and efficiently. That oil is *data*, and the data is further enhanced and maximized by automation and AI.

AUTOMATION AND AI

This is where things get interesting but also controversial. In our industry, when you start talking automation and AI, one of two things happen: either people get really, really excited, or they get really, really timid and frightened (it's that fear of the unknown and fear of change, once again). The number one question I get—in marketing but even more so in sales—around these subjects: "Is my job safe?" People want to know whether they are going to be replaced by a robot.

What I tell them, first of all, is to **turn off the news**. When we hear about automation and AI in the news, it's almost all fear-mongering. Why is that? Because it's the news! It's *designed* to play to your fears. That's how it keeps your attention.

The truth about automation and AI is much more nuanced than what you hear in the media. Think about all the jobs yet to come because of this technology. There's so much we can't even *begin* to fathom. Think about all you'll be able to do. This is what it means to move from a legacy mindset into a growth mindset. Whether you're coming from a marketing perspective, sales perspective, or executive perspective, you should be *excited* by the opportunities created through automation and AI. Your best days are still ahead of you.

In this new world built around automation and AI, there will be much more emphasis on our ability to *learn*, *think*, and *review* and less on our ability to *do*, because the latter operational domain will be handled increasingly by machines.

This is what marketing of the future will look like: all the repeatable tasks and processes that can be done better by a machine will finally be taken off our plates. But wait, don't relax and enjoy yourself a drink like Don Draper from *Mad Men* just yet.

On the human side of marketing, what will be most important is critical thinking and problem solving. In this way, we will transform marketing for the better and fundamentally change how we are perceived. Instead of being viewed as kids who play with paint and crayons, marketing teams will be seen as *experience engineers* who use creative thinking to solve complex problems and design memorable experiences.

Technology, and particularly automation and AI, will help us do that.

> Don't fear AI. Instead, look at it as a way to make yourself smarter, better, faster.

To quote Rob High, the chief technology officer at IBM Watson: "Cognitive technology, that's AI and automation, is there to extend and amplify human expertise, not replace it."

When I look at technology, I see it not as a human replacement but a human upgrade. We have two choices: either we can try to master it—using the technology to bring together two humans, the consumer and the guide—or we can let technology master us.

Remember, the fundamental opportunity is to help guide people beyond the financial stress that's keeping them up at night and taking such a heavy toll on their health and relationships. The goal is to get them to a bigger, better, and brighter future.

There's a lot to be learned, too, from this quote by Matthew Upchurch, CEO of the luxury travel company Virtuoso: "We need to look to automate the predictable and humanize the exceptional." That insight is itself built on the idea from Issy Sharp, founder of Four Seasons Hotels and Resorts, that we should "systemize the predictable and humanize the exceptional."

All of this is really just a modern-day take on ancient wisdom about experience. But it's especially powerful coming from Sharp, given the Four Seasons' well-deserved reputation around consumer experience.

An experience is nothing more than a set of systems and processes—centered on the digital consumer journey—that have been defined, applied, and optimized over time resulting in a positive or negative emotion.

Returning to the Digital Growth Engine, let's look now at how automation and AI create opportunities in each of the four gears.

First, when it comes to targeted ads and emails (i.e., building an audience, or step one in the BANCER Strategy Circle), this is really where the data comes into play. You have data around (a) website behavior (what are people looking at on our financial brand websites?) and (b) purchase behavior (what financial products of ours do people have, what are people buying at stores, where are they shopping frequently, and what are the most common patterns and trends in their spending habits?). Then there is one more data element in relation to targeted ads and emails, which has to do with (c) third-party bank fees. What are the possible opportunities for third-party ATM fees aggregated via a personal financial management (PFM) platform? Maybe you can find people sending and paying a third-party financial brand for a loan or credit card. Why don't we make these people an offer to help improve their financial situation beyond what it is today?

With all three of these examples (website data, purchase data, and data around third-party fees), we need to use automation, AI, machine learning, and so forth to identify where opportunities exist. It would be impossible otherwise; the data sets are too huge.

Once again, the goal is just to identify trends, patterns, and associations and within those, find the opportunities. It's important to remind ourselves *why* we are doing all of this in the first place. It's easy to lose ourselves in the data, all the ones and zeros, and forget the human context. We must remember **we're trying to elevate the digital experience— using data, automation, and AI as a human upgrade**.

The legacy marketing systems of the past (built on sending direct mail, placing newspapers ads, or running TV and radio ads) were taking a *reactive* stance in the marketplace—that is, waiting for something to happen. But now, through data, automation, and AI, we're able to take a *proactive* stance in our consumer's financial life. Especially if we can take an empathetic tone in our communication and messaging strategies, it shows the consumer that we care.

I first saw the power of this back when I was working at Old Navy. By simply taking a proactive stance in someone's shopping experience—standing at the front of the store with a blue Old Navy bag, greeting the person when they came in and offering to walk them around the store, guiding them and holding the bag as we shopped *with* them—we became the number one-selling Old Navy in the country for three years straight!

We certainly wouldn't have had that success if we had just stood back waiting for the customer to come to us. It wasn't brain surgery; it was just basic marketing and sales strategy centered on people. And the same logic applies in digital where you're just now using technology to connect two human beings together.

It's this kind of thinking we apply when we take these data sets and use them to build audiences. For example, maybe we try to identify ideal account holders who are in need of a credit card based on spending and credit data. Or perhaps we target consumers who have a checking account but not an auto loan, even though we see them paying a third-party auto lender every month. There is even an opportunity to use data to reduce attrition by proactively engaging and reaching out to consumers who may be close to heading out the door and closing their account.

The point is that once we've identified and built these audiences and then segmented our list, we have the opportunity to *proactively* send automated emails to them. Furthermore, in addition to sending proactive emails, you can also place and run digital ads against your segmented, highly targeted list to create multichannel digital touch points. You do this by integrating data with third-party platforms like Facebook, Instagram, LinkedIn, Google, and YouTube.

But we have to remember to *help first and sell second*. Don't just promote the product. Again, what people are looking for most is help, hope, and guidance. They want shortcuts and solutions to solve their problems. Your financial products are nothing more than a means to an end.

> Help first and sell second to guide people to a bigger, better, and brighter future.

This is how automation and AI create opportunities with targeted emails and targeted ads. What about the second gear of the Digital Growth Engine, the website itself?

USING AUTOMATION AND AI WITH YOUR WEBSITE

Here, we see how automated optimization—with proactive content—serves our needs for attracting leads with personalized offers (step two in the BANCER Strategy Circle). When it comes to personalization, there are two different options: one is **rule-based targeting** and the other is **automated one-to-one personalization**.

Rule-based targeting involves defining rule sets. For example, say you have a homebuyer who has previously visited the home-buying pages or mortgage pages on your website. You see that they have viewed three or more mortgage pages in the last seven days. Now you can take some kind of action. This approach—rule-based targeting—is very powerful, particularly when you have some historical data. As marketer, it gives you a very fine-grained control over the content you're proactively delivering. It gives **context behind the content** you are sharing with the consumer. But this approach can be hard to scale, especially when you're having to constantly adjust rule sets as consumer behavior changes.

That's where the second option can be useful. Automated one-to-one personalization with website content means looking at automation to create dozens of different user experiences and then letting the algorithms decide when to feature each one. The only problem here is that it's probably not the most winning experience for the consumer. For example, when shopping for a new auto loan, maybe someone is browsing for a certain type of car. Now, for the next few months, they're going to be followed around the web with that car they were looking for, sometimes even after they've purchased the car.

Both of these tools—rule-based targeting and automated one-to-one personalization—can be useful. It all comes down to what's best for your unique situation.

Applying this type of automation for website personalization and content is all about looking at, recommending, and predicting personalized content or offers. It's about web experiences that are contextualized with customized imagery and text (like headline and call to action) based on data from the person's previous website visit or from your core system where *all* your customer data is kept—or even from looking at third-party transactional data.

For example, instead of the rotating banner on your homepage—which, as mentioned earlier, is really a holdover from the legacy days of billboard one-to-many messaging—you can use that same real estate for personalization. You simply personalize a message for when the consumer returns to the website. Let's say they were looking at your mortgage pages. Now you can give them something of value by serving up an offer to download a home-buying guide.

That's a perfect example of how to use automation and AI to contextualize and personalize website concepts. But what about marketing automation, the third gear of the Digital Growth Engine?

MARKETING AUTOMATION

Here's the issue: in the banking space, marketing automation is often viewed through the lens of a post-conversion activity to onboard and cross-sell accounts. Nothing wrong with this perspective, as it does create value further down in the consumer buying journey. But where *we*'re looking at marketing automation is through the lens of the Digital Growth Engine—that is, higher up in the consumer buying journey. We're interested in how marketing automation integrates directly with the website to capture and nurture leads coming in from the site.

This, then, takes us back to step three in the BANCER Strategy Circle of nurturing leads with marketing automation and content. **The number one goal of a website is to generate leads, but not all leads are created equal.** That's because each lead is at a different stage of the buying journey. But with marketing automation, we can utilize this technology to send the right content at the right time based on where the person is in their buying journey. We can also route the right leads to the right people internally, to get one human being connected with another as early on in that buying journey as possible.

This is important because the faster we create a human connection—higher up or further along in the buying journey—the higher the propensity for conversion. This is true even when the human connection or interaction is an automated experience.

Unfortunately, our research tells us about 70 percent of financial brands still to this day do not have a marketing automation platform as a key part of their marketing technology stack. Moreover, as we learned in the previous chapter, 83 percent of financial brands do not have a strategy to follow up with abandoned applications—and through the Digital Secret Shopping Studies we've conducted, only 3 percent of financial brands actually followed up on an abandoned application with a phone call or email. This is not a promising number, considering 85 percent to 92 percent of online applications are indeed abandoned!

It is here we've identified one of the greatest opportunities for marketing and sales alignment. From a marketing automation practicality standpoint, deploying abandoned application follow-ups is an easy win. It's one of the best, quickest ways you can use marketing automation to create exponential value by generating digital leads for sales teams to follow up with.

> Seventy percent of financial brands do not have a marketing automation platform.

When it comes to abandoned applications, part of the underlying problem is financial brands are held hostage by poor third-party experiences. When someone tries to open an account online or apply for a loan and then abandons the application, often it's because of a broken digital experience—and that experience, unfortunately, is created and managed by the third party. But trying to get that third party to actually do something about it is like trying to get my kids to clean up their room: there's a lot of shouting and yelling on both sides, but then nothing happens. Or if I'm lucky enough that something *does* happen, still it takes way too long.

Thankfully, abandoned applications are a problem that can be solved, and all in all, we've seen great success when financial brands use marketing automation to address the problem. By deploying this technology and strategic thinking, they end up gaining 10 percent to 15 percent more loans and accounts from those users who had initially abandoned!

Clearly, there's real, bottom-line value to be created here. People appreciate when you take a proactive stance and follow up with them, whether an automated email or a phone call from an empathetic digital sales team member.

This is just one way marketing automation can serve to create value around one of the biggest problems I see in the consumer journey.

SALES AND SERVICE ENABLEMENT

Last but not least, let's look at how automation and AI work in sales and service enablement, the fourth gear of the Digital Growth Engine. This is where we're converting leads to loans and deposits, which is step four in the BANCER Strategy Circle. Here, CRM is at the core of any sales and service enablement strategy deployment.

As I mentioned earlier, traditionally CRM has been viewed as a challenge for financial brands. A lot of this stems from cultural resistance and particularly fear of change: people are scared to have to change the way they work. Often, they also just lack focus. They're trying to do too much at once. I've heard these lamentations so many times from marketing and sales teams. **Instead of talking about the *value* of CRM, they talk about it as a *cost* in terms of the pain and suffering that it's caused them.**

This is my recommendation when it comes to CRM: instead of looking at it as an organization-wide exercise, just focus on one specific area of opportunity or even one specific product line. Think of it more as a pilot program opportunity, not for the entire organization but just a smaller micro-digital sales team, who uses CRM simply to manage, nurture, and convert inbound digital leads coming from the website.

As your website continues to generate leads at an exponential pace, automation and AI can come in for both inbound and outbound sales activity. This is what really gets me excited about the future: we now have the ability (and this isn't just theory; there are already platforms on the market for this) to use an AI-driven virtual receptionist for call-answering coverage or chatbot with inbound digital leads. The AI is indistinguishable from a real human being.

AI then qualifies the lead, collects contact information, schedules appointments, creates new contact information in either the marketing automation or CRM platform, and logs the call or chat summary. Imagine how much time this frees up for you to not have to focus on every inbound lead. Then, for the inbound leads that are the hottest, of course you can get a human being involved at that point.

So that's the inbound side. But we can also look at AI to power outbound sales activity. For example, outbound AI can fully automate sales and marketing tasks by having conversations with both leads and account holders—to engage prospects who might have recently downloaded some marketing content (e.g., the home-buying guide). This helps to further qualify them. But again, what matters most is that by placing the outbound phone call, you're taking a proactive stance. Then, when you have a hot lead and need some more context and critical thinking around the buying journey, *that*'s when AI can transfer the lead to a human.

So those are just two examples of how automation and AI can be used in sales and service enablement. As you can see, it's not about replacing people with AI but rather using AI to get the right lead in touch with the right person at the right time. At one point or another, you *do* get a human being involved. It's all about context.

> AI helps you get the right lead in touch with the right person at the right time.

Now that you've seen how automation and AI can be applied through these four different lenses, four different gears of the Digital Growth Engine, let's look at what happens when a financial brand puts all of these tools together.

There was a financial brand we worked with, and they spent a lot of time developing their marketing automation work-flows, almost 200 of them. It took about eighteen months. They started very slowly and piloted the automated workflows with just one product to begin with. Then, once they created value through the marketing automation pilot program, they applied the strategic thinking across the board for every single one of their product lines.

After applying the strategic marketing automation workflows, this particular financial brand saw an 80 percent increase over the following four years in the number of digital leads they generated. From an email perspective, they saw open rates more than double as they were targeting the right people with the right messages. Most importantly, *conversation* rates increased: for one particular loan campaign, they closed 17 percent of digital leads generated.

For this financial brand, success came down to sending the right message, with the right content, at the right time in the buying journey. And the only way for them to deliver this was through AI and automation.

WHAT COMES NEXT

Now that you understand the Digital Growth Engine and the four different gears that power it, I want to take a deep dive into the website. We won't do this for each of the gears, but the website is really at the heart of the entire engine. It's a financial brand's primary future sales channel, the place where growth is going to come from, the e-commerce storefront.

Up to this point, investment in financial brand websites has been nominal. That must change now, as we will see in chapter eight.

* * * * *

WE WILL BUILD A WEBSITE THAT SELLS

Back in 2000, Toys "R" Us inked a ten-year contract to be the exclusive vendor of toys on Amazon. Similarly, Target had their own early agreement with Amazon, not to be a vendor but to have Amazon run their e-commerce operations.[27]

I bring up these two examples to highlight an important difference between them. It has to do with their websites. It took Toys "R" Us ten years to revamp the website that they had originally established in 2006. At the time of the revamp, in 2016, Toys "R" Us pledged to invest $100 million into its e-commerce efforts over the next three years. But by that point, it was too little too late.

We know what happened to Toys "R" Us. They didn't make it and filed for bankruptcy in 2017, forcing the closing of all of their physical stores. They were stuck in the present making decisions informed by past successes. Howard Davidowitz, a retail consultant with Toys "R" Us in the 1980s and 1990s,

---

27   Stephanie Pandolph, "Here's How Amazon May Have Led to Toys 'R' Us' Demise," Business Insider, September 20, 2017, https://www.businessinsider.com/ heres-how-amazon-may-have-led-toys-r-us-demise-2017-9.

noted during the 2017 bankruptcy, "Toys R Us, which had basically devolved into a warehouse, did not have the vision or the money to give its customers a great experience. For a toy store to survive, they've got to create the kind of fun that Amazon can't."[28]

In late 2019, Toys "R" Us attempted to make a comeback with smaller physical 6,500-square-foot locations (for comparison, legacy Toys "R" Us stores were typically about 40,000 square feet) built around "immersive experiences" to support an entirely revamped digital retail experience that is once again being outsourced, this time to Target. Is this history repeating itself? Did Toys "R" Us not learn one damn thing from the past? As Jason Goldberg, chief commerce strategy officer of Publicis Communications, notes, "If [Toys "R" Us] was truly trying to rebuild a sustainable toys business, they would never want to outsource their e-commerce to a third party and certainly not to a rival."[29]

Target, on the other hand, committed to shore up $2.5 billion per year to optimize its own online presence once their Amazon partnership agreement ended. Target knew that to compete with Amazon, they had to really ramp up their digital e-commerce business. That's why in March 2017, CEO Brian Cornell had the courage to invest over $7 billion in a turnaround strategy that would revamp the entire Target experience. Unlike the story of Walmart in chapter five, Target has invested in the future. Cornell noted, "We're investing in

28 Abha Bhattarai, "Toys R Us Is Back from the Dead, but Its New Stores Are Unrecognizable," *The Washington Post*, July 19, 2019, https://www.washingtonpost.com/business/2019/07/18/toys-r-us-is-back-dead-its-new-stores-are-unrecognizable/.

29 Anne D'Innocenzio, "Toys R Us Making a Comeback via Archrival Target," *USA Today*, October 9, 2019, https://www.usatoday.com/story/money/2019/10/08/toys-r-us-makes-target-run-reboot-ahead-holiday-shopping-season/3912351002/.

our business with a long-term view of years and decades, not months and quarters."[30]

Both Target and Toys "R" Us had an early relationship with Amazon. But only Target saw the opportunity in digital as the primary driver of growth going forward—and you can see this in the attention they pay to their website and its continual optimization of their digital shopping experience. Furthermore, instead of going directly head-to-head with Amazon and Walmart, Target has chosen to strategically combine the best of the digital and physical worlds together with their "ship-to-store" strategy.

This strategy enables Target to turn physical stores into mini warehouses for digital customers who can order a product online, pick it up in a store on the same day, and then do even more shopping if they need to—a strategy that drives additional revenue for Target. In fact, Target's physical stores are fulfilling more than half of their total digital volume through their "ship-to-store" offering.[31] Cornell stated additional benefits of the program, noting, "When delivered by stores as opposed to a distribution center, the cost of an order falls by 40 percent on average. When customers come to the store to pick up orders on top of that...90 percent of the eCommerce-related costs go away."

The tragic tale of Toys "R" Us compared to the transformative tale of Target have many underlying lessons for financial

30 Justin Bariso, "Amazon Almost Killed Target. Then, Target Did the Impossible," *Inc.*, October 21, 2019, https://www.inc.com/justin-bariso/amazon-almost-killed-target-then-target-did-impossible.html.

31 Matt Lindner, "Target Says Stores Will Fulfill More than 80% of Its Online Orders over the Holidays," Digital Commerce 360, November 15, 2017, https://www.digitalcommerce360.com/2017/11/15/target-expects-stores-will-handle-80-online-orders-closer-holidays/.

brands. Unfortunately, most banks and credit unions operate more like Toys "R" Us than Target when it comes to investing in their websites and digital shopping experience. It takes them forever to iterate through different versions. This is a problem because if you wait ten years like Toys "R" Us to upgrade your website, well, by then everything's changed: consumer behavior, competition, strategies, user experience, best practices, and more.

From our Digital Growth Diagnostic Assessments as well as from conducting what now total over 1,200 different Digital Secret Shopping Studies with a primary focus on lead and emotional experience for financial brands, we can safely say that almost across the board in our industry, **financial brand websites are nothing more than glorified online brochures**.

Sure, if a website has been updated within the past year, it might look a little better from a design perspective. It might function better—that is, be more mobile responsive. Hopefully, the website is at least ADA compliant, which is a requirement and standard now. But from a strategic functionality perspective, it's very likely the website is no better than it was. It's certainly not the Digital Growth Engine it has the potential to be.

WHY ARE FINANCIAL BRAND WEBSITES BROKEN?

Who's to blame for this sad state of affairs? To me, the biggest problem is that when it comes to their websites, financial brands typically just *self-diagnose*. They create a list of features that *they*, as a financial brand, want the website to have. Many times, a financial brand's "website wish list" is driven by the leadership team informed by the past and operating in the present moment, not the future.

The problem is that when you *self*-diagnose, more than likely you are going to *mis*diagnose. Imagine going to the doctor and telling them, "I want this, this, and this because I've already figured out what my problem is." They would look at you like you were crazy!

> Most financial websites are nothing more than glorified online brochures.

Once, we conducted a Digital Growth Diagnostic Assessment with a financial brand who had just launched their website thirty to sixty days earlier. After assessing and diagnosing the situation, we had to go back and deliver bad news: "You just invested six figures into your new website, and all you got out of it was a glorified online brochure that is now ADA compliant. Here's why." It was not a pleasant conversation, as the website was built following a list of requirements and needs set by and for the leadership team, not consumers and potential account holders.

This is what happens when you make the mistake of self-diagnosing. It leads to misinformed decisions based on what *you* need, or what you think you need, as a financial brand—when **you should really be viewing your website through the lens of consumers and *their* buying journey**.

Another big part of the problem here has to do with *funding*, particularly the lack of it for financial brand websites. Consider that to build a physical branch location, financial brands will spend between $2.5 and $5 million. Then, on top of that, it takes between $500,000 to $750,000 a year just to operate the branch.

According to an industry study by Peak Performance as reported by *The Financial Brand*, "Just slightly more than half (52%) of all branches in the banking industry are achieving acceptable levels of profitability. Over one quarter (28%) are below breakeven, and most of the remainder are at least contributing to overhead even if they are not achieving acceptable ROI. That might be tolerable if unprofitable branches were growing at a sufficient rate to become profitable down the road, but they aren't. **Half of the branches that are unprofitable today will never cross the breakeven threshold; they will forever be a drain on resources.**"[32]

Meanwhile, the average amount a financial brand will invest to build a new website, according to our year-over-year studies, is only $32,714. There's not any correlation with website investment and asset size: many larger asset institutions are also underfunding their website investments because their websites are still being viewed internally as just an information source (i.e., glorified online brochure), not a driver of growth.

Only around 13 percent of financial brands we've surveyed in our annual studies have invested more than $80,000 to build a new website. When you think about it, even $80,000 is a drop in the bucket compared to what they spend to build a physical branch. But how long will it take for that branch to become profitable? Will it even ever break even?

Once again, let's recall the tragic and transformative tales above. Target committed $7 billion to optimize their entire digital shopping experience, whereas Toys "R" Us pledged a

---

32   Guenther Hartfeil, "Are Your Bank's Branches Too Small to Survive?" *The Financial Brand*, August 21, 2018, https://thefinancialbrand.com/74386/bank-branch-roi-deposits-profitability/.

paltry $100 million into its e-commerce efforts. Learn from the failures of others that have gone before you. Who will your financial brand be more like in the months and years to come?

We must put the digital consumer journey at the center of all of our thinking and doing. As noted in the previous chapter, 87 percent of consumers start their buying journeys for financial products online. And with the in-person, in-branch experience currently having the highest pull-through and conversion rate for digital leads, **lead generation must be the number one goal of the website in the first place, regardless of whether the lead converts online, over the phone, or in the branch.**

This is why digital growth is not just about marketing but also about marketing and sales *working together*.

> Marketing generates the digital leads. Sales nurtures and closes them.

TRANSFORM A GLORIFIED ONLINE BROCHURE INTO A WEBSITE THAT SELLS

Through our own industry studies, we've found, on average, that financial brands build a new website every four to seven years, and with each of these cycles, there's an average twelve- to eighteen-month period where you're just building the new site. Worst of all, the actual value the site then creates is minuscule. As the graph illustrates, the impact of the website is stairstepped: time continues to expand, but in terms of value creation, it's almost like you're stuck in time.

It just shows how off-base we are in terms of how we're looking at these websites across the entire industry. We have it all wrong, from budget to build to go-to-market strategies.

GROWTH-DRIVEN DESIGN

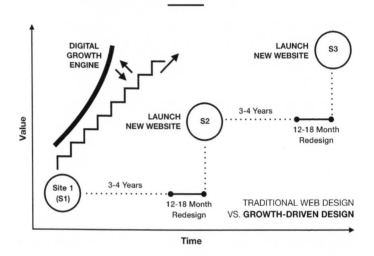

So what's the solution? In order to build *a website that sells*, you have to focus on growth-driven design. That means getting a foundational website out in the marketplace in about six months, as opposed to the usual twelve to eighteen months. How? Think minimal viable product (MVP) used to collect the maximum amount of real-world data and insights about consumer behavior with the least amount of effort and investment. The strategic framework for a website that sells must be informed by digital consumer studies and research that can be benchmarked against previous iterations of the website. Then, once you bring a website that sells to market, you optimize the website every quarter based on qualitative and quantitative data.

This means conducting ongoing Digital Secret Shopping Studies every ninety days that are framed around your website's lead experiences and emotional experiences. Consider consumer interviews, user recordings of landing pages, heat maps, click maps, conversion funnels, and so on. I know this sounds overwhelming, but you don't have to optimize the entire website all at once. **Just commit to focusing on one key product line each quarter and how you can create more value around it for consumers on your website.**

Pay attention to the language you use internally: stop thinking about your website as *the website*, and instead start thinking about your website as just one gear that makes up the Digital Growth Engine.

Break down your website into smaller pieces—individual digital consumer journeys and sales funnels for each product line—so your efforts are easier to comprehend and manage. Otherwise, optimizing your website will feel like an overwhelming beast you'll never defeat.

You also don't need to wait to build an entirely new website to apply these insights. There's no better time to start optimizing your website than now. For example, you could commit to spend ninety days focusing on optimizing your mortgage buying experience on your website. Then, in the next ninety-day period, you could focus on optimizing the checking shopping experience. Then credit cards, auto...You get the picture.

Regardless if you start optimizing your website now or wait to build a new one, be sure to set goals for growth. All too often, when building a new website, we find financial brands lack defined goals. We see this all the time in the diagnostic work we do. What do these banks and credit unions actually want from their website: do they want more traffic, more leads? What is their benchmark of what success looks like? If you don't have the proper analytics in place now, you can't establish benchmarks, as there's no way to measure bottom-line performance on previous iterations of your website.

> If you don't have proper analytics in place, you can't benchmark website performance.

ELIMINATE CONTENT COMPLEXITY AND CALL-TO-ACTION CONFUSION TO INCREASE CONVERSIONS

The Financial Brand shared a study by Change Sciences that examined how banking websites scored for usability and happiness. The results were shocking: consumer banking websites have the lowest conversion rates of all industries and the lowest perceived happiness of all financial verticals.[33]

This means financial brand websites today have a lot of content—complex and jargon-filled content—that leads to increased consumer confusion. Remember we talked about how iconography helps to ease the pressure of cognitive load? I recommend **reducing the text, consolidating content pages, and replacing copy blocks and bullet points with visualized imagery and iconography**.

Furthermore, if an increase in complexity and cognitive load

---

33 Jeffry Pilcher, "What Do Consumers Really Want from Banking Websites? Simplicity," *The Financial Brand*, February 13, 2014, https://thefinancialbrand.com/34825/banking-website-design-simplicity-research/.

through jargon-filled content wasn't enough, there is also consumer confusion around financial brand website calls to action (CTAs). That's because the majority of financial brand website CTAs are only for those consumers that are ready to apply for a loan or open an account. What about CTAs for consumers who are in the consideration stage of their consumer buying journey?

As shared by Digital Banking Report, 98 percent of consumers do NOT convert on their first visit.[34] That's because there are no conversion points for those who are just starting their shopping journeys for financial products! The solution is to add transitional CTAs on your website to help consumers transition from one stage of the buying journey to the next. Through our ongoing testing and studies, we've found transitional CTAs that work well include "Request a Callback" or "Schedule a Meeting."

When adding exponential CTAs to your website that will generate exponential leads, it is important to consider how your website that sells can be integrated with a marketing automation platform to capture and nurture leads for loans and deposits, as we discussed in chapter seven.

Through our Digital Secret Shopping Studies, we consistently see trends that reinforce the data around consumer content complexity and CTA confusion. For example, we recently performed an initial benchmark study for a financial brand and found they had a digital Net Promotor Score of only four out of ten for their entire website experience. Their mortgage

---

34 Jim Marous, "Retargeting—Everything Banks and Credit Unions Need to Know," *The Financial Brand*, February 25, 2018, https://thefinancialbrand.com/34921/online-digital-retargeting-for-banks-credit-unions-jm/.

shopping experience rated even worse, with a Net Promoter Score of only two. Auto was a four. The only experience that got a semi-decent score of seven was for their checking.

When we helped oversee the launch of their new website, the website strategies we recommended focused on two things: reducing cognitive load by cutting content and increasing opportunities for consumers to convert throughout the entire website. We did this with specific CTAs positioned around *helping first, selling second.* Ultimately, this financial brand improved their overall website Net Promoter Score to an eight, their mortgage Net Promoter Score and shopping experience score to an eight, their checking to an eight, and their auto to a ten! In only twelve months, they saw their digital lead conversions increase by about 300 percent.

Notably, they also drastically *simplified content* through consolidation and elimination, reducing the number of pages on their website by 80 percent to 85 percent. **Instead of user experience driving the content experience, content drove the user experience.**

That matters because historically, content has driven a website's user experience leaving financial brands locked in "content prisons" where content is typically communicated through blocks of text, paragraphs, and bullet points.

However, when you're building a *website that sells*, you create a content-first architecture and develop content modules that can be plugged in and moved around to lots of different places on the website. It's like building with Lego blocks. Content modules streamline future website optimizations while protecting the digital brand experience, as you have a library of content assets you can pull from. For example, you might have twenty or twenty-five of these different content modules that power your entire website, but they can be shifted around while the content is personalized based on product, persona, buying journey stage, and so on.

Content must inform and guide the website development process.

DIGITAL SECRET SHOPPING: THE SECRET TO CAPTURING 10X MORE DIGITAL LEADS

To build a website that sells, you must establish systems, processes, and habits rooted in ongoing optimizations that are informed by Digital Secret Shopping Studies. Recalling the operating insights from chapter five, every ninety days, you have to ask yourself, what am I testing this quarter? What will I make better? How can we improve our website to generate even more leads for loans and deposits? You could, for example, be testing your website's product pages, landing pages, or even the entire consumer journeys of digital marketing campaigns.

Through a recent industry study we conducted that included more than 300 financial brands, we found 94 percent of bank and credit union websites have never undergone any type of digital secret shopping testing. Alternatively, 72 percent of financial brands perform ongoing secret shopping studies for their physical branches. The lack of focus on digital secret shopping is troubling, as we know 87 percent of consumer journeys begin online regardless of where they apply.

The secret to conducting a successful Digital Secret Shopping

Study is to ask good questions. Here are a few examples from a library we've built over the years through our own experience conducting qualitative tests for financial brands:

- "Based on the page you viewed, do you feel like you can trust this financial brand?"

- "How does this mortgage page make you feel?"

- "What information do you feel is missing to help you make a decision?"

- "Imagine you're buying a home: What would you do next?"

- "Where else would you look to gain information when shopping for a mortgage?"

- "On a scale of 1 to 10, how likely would you be to refer your friend to this website based on your shopping experience?"

- "If you had a magic wand, what would you do to make this shopping experience better?"

You're also able to bring in competitive benchmarks, as you test not only on your financial brand's website but also gather data on the digital shopping experience (for, say, a mortgage product) against two to three competitors. Here you ask, "How helpful was financial brand A's shopping experience compared to financial brand B's shopping experience?"

After they walk you through what experience was more helpful, you wrap things up by saying, "Based on your shopping experience, if this wasn't a test, what financial brand would you choose to apply for your mortgage at and why?"

Digital Secret Shopping Studies are the secret to generating 10X more leads for loans and deposits because **you're letting consumers tell you exactly what they need from you to help guide them through their shopping journey.** Your website will improve exponentially over the course of just twelve months when you commit to conducting quarterly studies like we've described here. This approach is so much better than waiting four to seven years to make progress.

COMMON PITFALLS THAT KILL FINANCIAL BRAND WEBSITES

My number one recommendation for financial brand marketing, sales, and leadership teams wanting to transform a glorified online brochure into a website that sells is to not fall into the trap of thinking you're the expert.

I know you have ideas you'd like to see on your new website, but when it comes to building it, you are *not* the expert. Who is? The consumer. They can guide you and tell you exactly what *they* need and are looking for on the website because the consumer is looking for a financial expert, you and your financial brand, to guide them beyond their questions and concerns toward a bigger, better, and brighter future.

Just like Jiminy Cricket encouraged Pinocchio, "Let your conscience be your guide," I'd like you to always remember to "let the consumer be your guide" when it comes to building a website that sells.

Second, don't make the mistake of failing to identify website goals or benchmark performance as the primary goal of a website that sells is to generate leads.

> The primary goal of a website that sells is to generate leads.

Next, don't make the mistake of committing yourself to an unrealistic timeline or underfunded budget. You'll just get stuck and feel frustrated as you fail to move forward and make any real progress. Remember, launch your website with an MVP (minimum viable product), and then commit to optimize your website every ninety days with the insights you gain through quarterly Digital Secret Shopping Studies.

Finally—this one is the true death knell—don't make the mistake of thinking the website is done once it's launched. It's never done. Ongoing optimization is the secret to maximizing your future digital growth.

WHAT COMES NEXT

These are the main strategies to consider when transforming the operational model of how you build a website for your financial brand. Focus on the key points above, and you will distinguish yourself from other financial brands in the industry. Remember, 94 percent of bank and credit union websites have never undergone any type of digital secret shopping testing.

In fact, what I've proposed throughout this chapter is almost the opposite of what every financial brand has done up to this point, as the majority continue to secret shop their physical branch locations. Digital Secret Shopping Studies framed around emotional experience (EX) and lead experience (LX) is a complete transformation beyond the legacy model rooted in the physical world. As 87 percent of bank shopping journeys start online, one of the greatest opportunities for you and your financial brand is to invest time, dollars, effort, and energy into secret shopping the most important channel for all of your future growth—that is, the website—regardless of whether consumers apply online, over the phone, or in the branch.

As I shared in chapter four, one financial brand we've guided over the years has experienced a 1,500 percent increase in leads from their website by reducing the overall cognitive load—number of pages and content—and utilizing more visual imagery and iconography, as well as increasing the number of transitional calls to action exponentially. Their website went from being the lowest performing acquisition channel to outperforming all of their physical branch locations. These results are real.

If we look back through the book and think about how far we've come, we'll see that we've not only established a strong foundation (in part one)—looking at and identifying purpose, personas, optimizing product positioning for digital, and establishing team and operational processes—but we've also now started to create quantifiable value by building a Digital Growth Engine.

Once you've built a Digital Growth Engine centered on a website that sells with marketing automation integration, we can now begin to drive traffic to your website. But you must first ensure you have the proper website conversion systems, including transitional CTAs along with abandoned application processes, in place. Otherwise, you risk wasting money and losing leads from the traffic you send to your website.

Once again, this all takes time. You're not going to build a Digital Growth Engine overnight. Instead, when you're strategizing and planning to build a Digital Growth Engine, consider implementing pilot programs as you continuously learn, think, do, and review while measuring progress, not perfection, every ninety days.

———

PART THREE

MAXIMIZE YOUR DIGITAL GROWTH POTENTIAL

At this point, you've got your website that sells. You've got your marketing automation system set up. Other technologies are now in play. It's time for you to turn on the gas and start driving traffic into your Digital Growth Engine.

Optimizing your Digital Growth Engine means maximizing your future digital growth potential by generating even more leads for loans and deposits.

You have the tools, the website that sells, the marketing automation. But now you need to actually turn your engine on—with some fuel.

The fuel of your Digital Growth Engine, as we have learned, is *content.*

And you can use content to tell stories—stories that sell.

CHAPTER NINE

* * * * *

WE WILL BE THE HELPFUL AND EMPATHETIC GUIDE

In the 1980s, there was a famous Duracell commercial—I used to see this all the time as a kid—featuring a bunch of toy bunnies banging on cymbals. Meanwhile, the voice-over in the ad is talking about how "Duracell lasts longer." Gradually, we see the bunnies all run out of batteries. Only one is still chugging along—the one, we assume, with the Duracell battery.

That's how Duracell positioned their product back in the 1980s as they promoted product features. But then in 2014, they launched a new commercial, produced by Saatchi & Saatchi New York, that touched the hearts of 5.9 million people in just two weeks after it launched on YouTube.[35]

The video begins with someone saying, "They told me it couldn't be done, that I was a lost cause. I was picked on and picked last. The coaches didn't know how to talk to me."

---

35 Grace Chung, "Duracell's Bet on Seahawks' Derrick Coleman Pays Off on Viral Chart," AdAge, January 22, 2014, https://adage.com/article/the-viral-video-chart/duracell-s-bet-seahawks-coleman-pays-viral-chart/291208.

Eventually, we learn this is the voice of Derrick Coleman, who played for the Seattle Seahawks. Coleman is the **first legally deaf offensive player in the NFL**.

In retrospect, what made the story so effective was the deep human emotion. Coleman's monologue became even more powerful when he said, "They gave up on me; they told me that I should just quit. They didn't call my name at the NFL draft. They told me it was over."

Man, I'm getting goose bumps just thinking about it!

The Coleman clip was originally intended for web-only distribution, but because of its emotional appeal and human connection, Duracell decided to run it as a TV ad during Super Bowl XLVIII. That year, Coleman's Seahawks went on to defeat the Denver Broncos.

Since 2014, Coleman's story has now been viewed tens of millions of times on YouTube. I've also showed this ad numerous times at conferences and workshops because it really hits home with people—especially the part, the transition point in the speech, where Coleman says, "But I've been deaf since I was three, so I did not listen." At the end of the commercial, Coleman wraps it all up with this: "And now I'm here, with a lot of fans in the NFL cheering me on and I can hear them all."

End scene. Duracell battery comes on: "Trust the power within."

> How does Derrick Coleman's Duracell story differ from the 1980s Duracell ad?

I like to compare and contrast these two Duracell commercials, from two different eras, because the earlier ad is about features, facts, and figures (Duracell "lasts longer" than, it is implied, Energizer), whereas the latter is really trying to tap into and tug at your heartstrings. Put more scientifically, the first ad is aimed at your neocortex with logic and reason; the second uses the secret power of story and narrative to light up your brain's limbic system with feelings and emotions.

Taking a step back, you could even say Coleman's story is trying to connect to the reptilian part of your brain by asking for your *trust*. If the story can get some emotional pull and create an empathetic connection through the message it communicates, it becomes far more likely a level of trust will also be established.

Throughout Coleman's story, the viewer is very much connecting with Coleman the human being—not the commoditized product, not the battery. Viewers can connect with how this professional athlete used the product, the battery, to overcome the "monster"—that is, the challenges of being deaf—and achieve his hopes and dreams.

What does all this have to do with financial brands? For years, I've heard speakers at industry conferences tell bank and credit union leaders that they have to "tell a better story." I'd sit there thinking, "What the hell does that even mean?" I became really frustrated because even though I agreed with the recommendation, it felt toothless. There was no substance behind it, no practicality.

How do you tell a better story?

The heart of the matter is, from a marketing communication standpoint, financial brand stories have not changed over the years. For the majority of banks and credit unions, the "story" can be distilled into three things: promoting "great rates," announcing "amazing service," and communicating commoditized laundry lists of look-alike product features.

It's not just that this is a *bad* story (because there is, in fact, *no* story here when you get down to it). It's more than that. There's a very specific problem with the traditional messaging and communications patterns here—namely, **this "story" is all about *us*, the financial brand**.

It's time to step outside of yourself and let go of your ego.

THE NARCISSISTIC MARKETING MODEL

What I call the narcissistic marketing model is really a hold-over from the legacy days of broadcast marketing. Narcissistic marketing is when a financial institution may have a solution to a problem for a mass market that might be called to action.

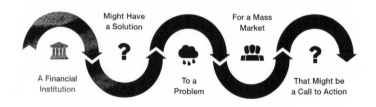

THE PROBLEM:
NARCISSISTIC MARKETING

But how exactly do they summon that call? In the traditional narcissistic narrative structure, financial brands position *themselves* as the hero.

What's so bad about that? you may wonder. Stop for a moment and think back to your ninth-grade or tenth-grade literature class. Even if you know very little about literary history, you probably understand that in every classic adventure or epic poem, there's room for only one hero. If you add a second hero to the story structure, that person usually becomes the antihero—the antagonist, rather than protagonist.

When I work with financial brand leadership teams in training sessions or strategy workshops, I hit this message hard. I tell them, "Guys, you're not the hero. You can't be the hero."

> In every story, there's room for only one hero. And the hero can't be you.

Now, if you're still having a hard time with this concept, may I suggest you think back on your own life and the different stages or scenes within your own story. We all walk around believing we're the hero in the narratives we tell ourselves, which is fair—**we *are* the heroes of *our own* story**.

But we're *not* necessarily the hero in other people's stories. Remember that old song by Bonnie Tyler that goes: "I need a hero / I'm holding out for a hero till the end of the night." Well, she was wrong about that. The message of that song is *not* very accurate. The truth is that people aren't looking so much for a hero externally—definitely not when it comes to financial services. They're looking for something greater, something deeper.

We can learn so much, and ultimately transform our marketing and sales communication strategies, by looking back over thousands of years of literary history, all the way to the earliest recorded narratives. Joseph Campbell studied this lineage and in 1949 came out with a book called *The Hero with a Thousand Faces*, where he essentially mapped out an archetypal narrative structure, identifying common patterns in the way stories have been told and communicated through the ages.

Why is it so important to understand these narrative structures?

When it comes down to it, humans respond to stories, not just intellectually but also emotionally. Stories have bonded us together as human beings through the course of our existence as a species. Stories are key to our survival. They are embedded in our DNA—or, if you prefer, buried in our soul.

The best stories worth telling and remembering have a point of conflict, and these are the perfect moments to try to get someone to *focus in*. It's during these points of conflict that our brains produce **cortisol**, increasing focus. Conflict captures attention.

On the flip side of cortisol is **oxytocin**, the "feel-good chemical" that promotes connection and empathy. This chemical is released in our brains when we see people's *faces* and their emotional reactions within a story. This is even more true when we see faces of people who look like us. This is why telling a story visually, through images and video, can create such a powerful empathetic connection through emotional experiences.

Finally, we know there is a secret power that can be unlocked within a story's *happy ending.* Because happy endings to a story trigger the limbic system to release **dopamine**, which in turn helps us feel more hopeful and optimistic.

THE HERO AND THE GUIDE

If we take Joseph Campbell's hero's journey framework and distill it into a more simplistic structure through the lens of financial brand marketing and sales strategies, we see the following key thematic elements:

- A hero has a problem

- Who meets a helpful and empathetic guide

- Who offers the hero a plan that provides clarity and builds their courage

- Which leads the hero to commit to take action with confidence

- Which ultimately results in the hero's success

Let's just briefly look and see how this simplified hero's journey pattern shows up, over and over again, in almost every Hollywood blockbuster. Think back to *Star Wars:* you've got the hero, Luke Skywalker, *who has a problem*: his father and the evil empire. Luke then *meets a helpful and empathetic guide,* Obi-Wan Kenobi, who *offers the hero a plan.* He teaches Luke the ways of the Force providing *clarity* and building Luke's *courage*. Luke eventually *commits to take action with confidence* when he blows up the Death Star, *which ultimately results in the hero's success.*

Classic George Lucas films aside, what I hope you take from this discussion, above all, is **every story worth telling, remembering, and sharing has two key roles: there's the hero, of course, but then there's also the helpful and empathetic guide.**

Without the guide, there can be no hero, and without the hero, there can be no story. Without Obi-Wan, there is no Luke and therefore no *Star Wars*. Without Mr. Miyagi, there is no Daniel-san and therefore no *Karate Kid*. And without Gandalf, there can be no Frodo and therefore no *The Lord of the Rings*.

In the example of Derrick Coleman's story, the guide in the commercial wasn't even a human being but a nonliving thing. The guide in Coleman's hero's journey was a battery that powered him, literally, helping to build his courage so Coleman could commit to take action with confidence, which ultimately resulted in his success—playing in the NFL.

As always, human or not, the guide's primary role in any story is to empathetically connect with and then empower and elevate the hero on their journey. Remember, empathy is the antithesis of narcissism. This means that **your financial brand can no longer position itself, within its marketing and sales communication, as the *hero*. You must commit to position your financial brand as the *helpful and empathetic guide*.**

> Empathy is the antithesis of narcissism.

As John Kotter of the Harvard Business School once shared with *Forbes*, "Leaders who understand this and use this knowledge to help make their organizations great are the ones we admire and wish others would emulate. Those in leadership positions who fail to grasp or use the power of stories risk failure for their companies and for themselves."[36]

TELL STORIES THAT SELL WITH STORYSELLING

Clearly, financial brand executives would be wise to heed Kotter's advice. But how do you escape the narcissistic marketing and sales communication that centers your financial brand as the hero? How do you begin to tell stories and position your financial brand as the helpful guide? More importantly, how do you tell stories that sell? Because let's be honest, from a leadership perspective, what good are the stories we tell if the stories don't generate leads for loans and deposits?

Your financial brand can confidently and consistently tell stories that sell by following the seven simple steps of the following StorySelling Method:

---

36 John Kotter, "The Power of Stories," *Forbes*, July 13, 2012, https://www.forbes.com/2006/04/12/power-of-stories-oped-cx_jk_0412kotter.html#4b0781ad6aee.

THE STORYSELLING METHOD

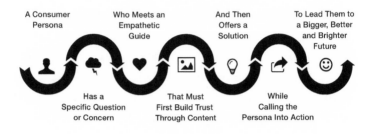

| A Consumer Persona | Who Meets an Empathetic Guide | And Then Offers a Solution | To Lead Them to a Bigger, Better and Brighter Future |

| Has a Specific Question or Concern | That Must First Build Trust Through Content | While Calling the Persona Into Action |

| AWARENESS | CONSIDERATION | PURCHASE |

1. **A consumer persona:** Who is the ideal consumer your story will emotionally connect with most? Remember, *focus is your friend* here. Don't try to be all things to all people and end up being nothing to no one. Look back to chapter three to review how to empathize with consumer personas.

2. **Has a specific question or concern:** This is where you lean into the consumer persona's pain as you establish conflict other people will be able to connect with. For example, what's keeping people up at night? How are they feeling about money? Reflect on these points from chapter three as you stir up negative emotion here—but only just a bit—because *conflict captures consumers' attention* as they realize they too need a cure to the pain they've now related to.

3. **Who meets an empathetic guide:** Enter your financial brand with empathy, as empathy is the antithesis of narcissism. This is why *positioning around purpose* is truly a

strategic competitive advantage in a commoditized marketplace, as we discussed in chapter two. People don't buy what you do or how you do it; those are easily commoditized. People buy why you do it.

4. **Who must first build trust through content:** Just like Luke didn't trust Obi-Wan—a weird, old hermit living alone in the desert of Tatooine—at first, why should a consumer trust you pushing your commoditized products on them? Trust is built on two things: (a) communication (what you say) and (b) action (what you do). And the way you build trust digitally is through the production (chapter ten) and promotion (chapter eleven) of content that *helps first and sells second*. You can also refer back to chapter seven as content is the fuel of the Digital Growth Engine.

5. **And then offers a solution:** Once, and only once, you've established enough trust with a consumer through the content you produce and promote—content that, again, helps first and sells second—can you finally offer them a solution. This solution is *a prescription* to *cure the consumer problems and pain*. Refer back to chapter four for more insights on how to position your products beyond the bullet points.

6. **While calling the persona to action:** A hero—the consumer—will only take action once they have built up enough courage to commit to move forward with confidence. The calls to action (CTAs) in your story will differ based on the medium in which you are telling your story. Take your website, for example. To keep things simple, there are three types of website CTAs that build up consumer courage over time at every stage of their buying journey:

A. **Clarity CTAs** provide insight, guidance, and help early and often in the awareness stage a consumer's buying journey (e.g., "Download the home-buying guidebook").

B. **Transitional CTAs** are ideal for the consideration stage of the buying journey when a consumer needs to first talk to someone before they have enough courage and confidence to commit and click "apply" (e.g., "Request a call back to talk to someone").

C. **Direct CTAs** are only offered at the very end of the consumer buying journey once they've compared all their options and built up enough courage and confidence to commit to move forward and apply with your financial brand (e.g., "Apply for your loan in less than five minutes").

7. **To lead them to a bigger, better, and brighter future:** It is here the hero has finally broken free from their past and has arrived at their new state of being. These are the happy endings you must highlight in the stories you tell about those you've helped, which will give hope to others. How? Consider the power of testimonials communicated via videos and podcasts, or even ratings and reviews embedded on the product pages of your website. Remember, at the end of the day, all people truly want are two things: help and hope. And hope must often come before help, especially when a consumer is looking for someone they can trust to guide them beyond their questions and concerns.

APPLYING THE STORYSELLING METHOD

Human beings connect with stories about people like them. We quickly relate to average-Joe consumers who, with the help of an empathetic guide, get beyond their financial stress and realize their bigger, better, brighter future.

Although we've discussed the StorySelling Method applied primarily to your website, there are seven other ways to apply this strategic thinking to create value for marketing, sales, and leadership teams:

· Via **strategic planning**, meaning being able to communicate what your plan is and where you need to go next on your Digital Growth Journey.

· Via **digital consumer journey mapping**, as the StorySelling Method is mapped to the consumer buying journey.

· Via **user experience and lead experience** on your website, as in literally laying out pages utilizing the framework of the StorySelling Method.

· Via **email marketing and digital ads**, as it's usually through these channels that the hero meets the empathetic guide. We'll talk more in part three about both and how they fit in.

· Via **blog articles**, where you structure your content and communication around the StorySelling Method.

· Via a **sales system** for financial brand sales teams—that is, applying the StorySelling Method not just as a marketing communication strategy but also in your approach to all incoming digital leads. The purpose here is to empower your financial brand's sales teams to bridge the gap with marketing by tapping into content libraries full of stories of success to nurture, convert, and close more leads for loans and deposits.

STORYSELLING IN ACTION

When a digital sales team uses the StorySelling Method, they develop story libraries to pull from that relate to whatever financial product a prospective consumer may be interested in.

For example, let's say a couple is looking to buy their first home. Instead of just talking about the product features itself, the mortgage loan officer will share a story about how she helped someone just like the couple sitting in front of her. She might recount how the couple before, just like the one she is helping now, came to her with such-and-such specific questions and concerns, and how she listened to them and worked alongside them to solve these problems.

Maybe it took some time, but as she describes, she guided them every step of the way, through x, y, and z. Ultimately, she helped the couple buy the house they loved so that they could live the life they had always dreamed of.

In telling this *story of success* from the past, the mortgage loan officer is positioning herself as the helpful and empathetic guide to the couple sitting in front of her in the present moment—and she's doing it not by talking directly about *herself or her financial brand's commoditized products* but rather about how she helped the other couple that looks just like the prospects sitting in front of her.

That was a hypothetical example, but I see the StorySelling Method applied in real life all the time—and I see how well it works. Let's take SunTrust, for example, who came to market with a program that they called the onUp movement. They launched their first big ad at the Super Bowl. The TV spot went like this: it started by recognizing the pains, questions, and concerns people have around money. Gary Sinise did the voice-over as the commercial took what he was saying about financial stress and reinforced it with striking visuals.

The crux of the message was that *there was hope* and that managing your finances didn't have to feel so stressful. When they talked about hope, they meant hope to "Get onUp" to a better future by moving "onward and upward toward financial confidence." This has, in actuality, become SunTrust's organizational purpose—their strategic North Star.

All in all, I found it a very effective communication resource in how the ad followed the basic steps of the StorySelling Method. First, it connected emotionally with the viewer, then built some trust by playing the role of the helpful guide. Finally, the story had a call to action: it sent people to a website.

Call to action is a key part of StorySelling—and one that is, unfortunately, often forgotten. In the case of SunTrust and their onUp program, the call to action was to drive viewers to onup.com to "join the movement." Within the first day, they had more than 38,000 people sign up. At that point, there wasn't a lot of content on the site. But the content that *was* there was very much through the lens of guiding/helping. Then, once people joined the movement, there was another call to action, which was assessing their financial situation with a very simple ten-question quiz.

What SunTrust was doing was capturing information they could then use to follow up with consumers based on each individual's unique financial story (as portrayed through their answers to the ten questions). In fact, we tested this and saw how well it worked. If you were to answer the quiz from your perspective and me from mine, we would then receive a series of automated emails that were totally different from each other based on our distinct situations.

It doesn't matter that it's an algorithm analyzing each response. What matters is how this information is used to convey an empathetic and personalized human touch that a consumer so appreciates. I like to think of this almost like those old *Choose Your Own Adventure* books I used to read as a kid. As in that beloved children's series, we see there are multiple paths to a story—just like everyone's life journey is different.

The opportunity is to utilize technology to provide the *right* content at the *right* time with the *right* context in someone's own life journey and adventure. And wow, that's a transformative experience right there.

I loved what SunTrust did with that program, and I love how their CMO, Susan Johnson, puts it when she describes her organization: "Saying that we're purpose driven isn't real. You have to act and actually apply this, this type of thinking." Once again, this is how you build trust with people: through your actions and words, through what you say and what you do.

> SunTrust and onUp are a perfect example of the potential value created when you position around purpose while committing to take on the role of helpful and empathetic guide.

Increasing trust through consistent and personalized communication is exactly what SunTrust has done with onUp, and over time, their results far exceeded their expectations. In fact, they've built up an ever-growing digital community. Initially, 1 million people joined the onUp movement; not only that, but it all happened way more quickly than they had ever intended. (Originally, they'd forecasted signing up 600,000 people!) Once they hit that million mark, though, they set a new goal for 5 million people to join the onUp movement in five years—which, as of late 2019, they have now surpassed once again.

From our continued study of the program, it is clear why consumers continue to commit to join the onUp movement. Everything that drives the onUp experience is positioned around a purpose far greater than pushing products and powered by content that positions SunTrust as the helpful and empathetic guide for consumers in search of help and hope.

It will now be interesting to see the role onUp will play in the months and years to come, as SunTrust and BB&T merged to form Truist and become the sixth largest retail bank in the United States. I believe the future is bright for them in an ever-growing digital economy. From my early perspective, it appears they are committed to playing the role of the helpful and empathetic guide as informed by their new brand name, Truist—a playful spin on altruism meaning "the principle or practice of unselfish concern for or devotion to the welfare of others" (as opposed to egoism).

WHAT COMES NEXT

Now that you've been introduced to the StorySelling Method—and the many different ways you can apply this strategic thinking—you will learn in the coming chapter how to take your consumer persona (with all its specific questions and concerns) and use it to step into the all-important role for them as the helpful and empathetic guide.

As a guide, you must build trust. The way you do that is by producing content that *helps first and sells second*. In the hero's journey, the helpful guide is not just automatically trusted by the hero. This rings true to what we've all seen in movies as well, right? Once again, Luke did not immediately trust Obi-Wan. He didn't immediately trust Yoda. Rather, trust was built over time, through the **actions and communications** of those helpful allies.

Admittedly, actions may be hard to deliver digitally, but *communication* is everything, and it's the only way we can build trust with people we don't get to see in person.

In the following chapter, we look specifically at how to build trust through content. This is the crux of the StorySelling Method. Once you build that trust through content, only *then* can you offer a solution. Only *then*, as the helpful and empathetic guide, can you call your hero to action and ultimately lead them to a bigger, better, and brighter future.

CHAPTER TEN

* * * * *

WE WILL PRODUCE CONTENT THAT HELPS FIRST

The year is 1962. An American named Bill is in New Zealand when he comes across something he's never encountered before: a jogging club. Bill, who was clearly out of shape at the time, was invited for a jog and could barely keep up with the other runners—some who were twenty years his senior. It is there and then that Bill begins to see the value of jogging as a traditional fitness routine. Keep in mind that at the time, over fifty years ago, jogging and fitness was not a thing like it is today.

When Bill returned from his trip, back home to Portland, Oregon—where he also just happened to be the track coach at the University of Oregon—he began writing articles and books about jogging and how it could be utilized as part of a fitness program. One of his very first such publications was a four-page pamphlet called *The Joggers Manual*. This manual originally sought to help inform people how to literally jog. It described jogging as an activity that, in its most simple form, "is a bit more than a walk."

From the pamphlet came the book *Jogging*, which Bill wrote alongside cardiologist Waldo Harris. Published in 1966, the book sold well over 1 million copies in its first publication and helped to further popularize the sport.

Through his continued focus and commitment on content production that guided people along their fitness journey toward better health, Bill helped to slowly grow the trend of running in the United States and around the world. Ultimately, Bill Bowerman would go on to found one of the most well-known modern brands today, which is, of course, Nike.

It's unlikely Bill's original goal was to become a multimillionaire, back when he was pinning together those first pages of his jogging pamphlet. He simply wanted to promote a sport and a healthy way of life—an idea that he genuinely believed in.

I bring up this story to show how **the early founding of Nike was very much built on the *content***, and in fact, Nike has continued to use content to fuel their growth over the years, both from an educational standpoint as well as through inspirational narratives and stories. The brand is well known for addressing social causes in their content, and often these causes are somewhat controversial (or even very controversial).

> Content fuels the Digital Growth Engine and connects with people to offer help and hope.

I love to think about those humble early days of Nike because it really wasn't about the shoe back then—it was about *helping first and selling second*. That's another key takeaway here. It's how Nike built so much trust, especially given that running was not a popular activity when they started out.

Back in the late '60s and early '70s, no one knew much about jogging. The subject matter was confusing. In fact, people at that time thought jogging and distance running was unhealthy and even potentially dangerous. **It was through content and communication that Nike was able to help consumers understand the value jogging could offer them.** Without first providing help (how to jog) and hope (why jogging will improve your health so you live longer and happier), Nike would have never been able to go on and become the sports shoe and apparel empire it is today.

We see the same dynamic when it comes to money matters.

As you'll recall from chapter four, through our Digital Secret Shopping Studies, we have asked literally thousands of consumers a key question: "How does money make you feel?" From that huge data set, we've distilled their responses down to the three most common emotional expressions around money. Here they are again:

- "I feel **confused** about money. I know money is important, but I really don't know what I should be doing because I can't seem to save any money. I'm just clueless."

- "I feel **frustrated** about money because I've tried so many things to save money, but I'm not getting any traction. In fact, my situation is actually getting worse, as I'm getting more and more into debt."

- "I feel **overwhelmed and stressed** about money. That's

having a negative impact on my life, my health, my well-being, and my relationships. I feel angry and depressed all the time. The debt is just too much to bear at this point."

The good news is that people are looking for someone like you and your financial brand to be their trusted guide to help them to a bigger, better, and brighter future. You'll remember from the Facebook study noted earlier that 60 percent of millennials are looking for exactly that: they want partnership and guidance from their financial institution. In that same study, however, you'll also remember that only 8 percent of millennials *trust* financial institutions for that guidance.

The question is why? It comes back to the narcissistic marketing model we talked about in the previous chapter, where financial brands position themselves as the hero in the stories they tell by promoting the same commoditized products and services.

How, as a financial brand, can you learn to do *content* right? That's what we'll be looking at in this chapter. But first, let's get a lay of the land as it stands today. When we look at the kinds of content coming out of financial brands, the most common types of content production activities we see are primarily around a smattering of social media posts followed by blogging.

But are these activities even successful? What value are they creating?

Through our industry studies, we've found **89 percent of financial brands lack a defined content strategy**. And as a result, financial brands producing content are wasting time, effort, energy, and resources because they are not able to prove the value of their content marketing efforts.

WHAT IS CONTENT MARKETING?

Similar to other definitions that we've defined in this book, content marketing is nothing more than a well-defined process to produce and promote helpful content on a consistent basis to attract, capture, nurture, and convert leads for loans and deposits.

Content marketing helps you build trust with consumers by positioning your financial brand as the financial matters expert that guides people beyond their questions and concerns toward a bigger, better, brighter future.

As we saw in chapter nine, content is also central to the StorySelling Method.

And as we saw in chapter seven, from a technology standpoint, content is the fuel of the Digital Growth Engine. It's what makes the gears turn. Here, it's important to recognize too that content becomes more than just an analog activity of sitting down and writing. The opportunity for financial brand marketers is to **use automation and AI to amplify content production**.

Again, I want to reinforce that automation and AI will not replace human content marketing. It will only augment and enhance it and provide more value and opportunity for content production at scale.

AI and automation should only be used with content-related

tasks that are repetitive in nature or structured around operation. You have to look at the value in each case. If you're able to augment the production, then value for your financial brand comes from setting your content marketing strategy and looking for ways to inject more emotion and empathy into the content itself.

The real value is in looking for opportunities to merge AI and creativity. I call this content intelligence—how to understand and capture elements like emotional pull and tone or sentiment at both a macro and micro level.

Chase has had amazing success in this area. They have a five-year deal with a platform called Persado, which is content marketing driven by AI and automation. Persado crafts messages for maximum consumer impact, and they do this by looking at data, around six different factors:

- The **narrative,** or description of how the consumer's life will be better.

- The **emotion,** or underlying potential that makes this worthy of taking action

- The **descriptive,** or what gives the message its appeal to connect and attract

- The **call to action**, or the biggest reason for the consumer to act now

- The **formatting,** which covers everything from boldness to placement to pictures or imagery

- And finally, the **positioning**, or how you visually arrange everything together to create and deliver a positive digital experience

All of these items are of course done by algorithms. It's completely dynamic. Think of it like A/B testing on steroids—it's *fast*.

I find this all quite fascinating and exciting in the opportunities it presents. What Chase is doing is pretty next level, but there are many other practical applications easily available to you for using AI and automation to transcribe content from audio and speed up the writing process.

Furthermore, you can use AI and automation to reverse the flow of production—for example, to take a blog article and turn it into a video with no human producer. Instead, there are algorithms for reading the text, pulling out the key points, and creating a video with related headlines and imagery or clips.

You, the human being, still drive the strategy. But **you're letting AI informed by data produce the narrative based on real-time interactivity of what is and isn't working**.

Regardless of if you're looking to more advanced content marketing strategies powered by AI and automation to produce content at scale, or if you are just starting to establish a content marketing foundation, there are three goals that should drive all of your content thinking and strategy.

- **Connect** with people to build audiences, increase website traffic, and generate leads

- **Cultivate** and nurture relationships with those leads to build trust over time

- **Convert** leads for loans and deposits

> There are three primary goals of content marketing strategy: connect, cultivate, and convert.

CONNECT, CULTIVATE, AND CONVERT WITH FOUR CONTENT ARCHETYPES

Now let's consider what types of content your financial brand can produce through the five stages of the digital consumer buying journey, as shared in chapter six. It is here we'll begin to see how *content* and *context* are applied together.

To begin, you must first ask yourself—as shared above—what are the primary goals for the content I need to produce over the next ninety days? Start with the end in mind and work backward from there. Where I see financial brands fall short is when they say they need to start a blog, produce some videos, or ramp up social media content without any clear path of why they are committing to these activities in the first place.

CONTENT **PRODUCTION** ARCHETYPES

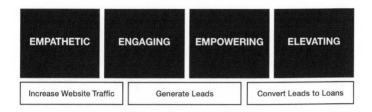

Once you identify the goal for content production—whether connecting, cultivating, or converting—you can then identify the types of content you need to produce. To do this well, approach this task guided by the following **four content archetypes** aligned to the digital consumer buying journey:

- **Empathetic:** this type of content is suitable when you're just trying to get consumers to like you in the first place. You need to show that you understand them at an emotional level so that they will trust you. This empathetic style and type of content is perfect for the early stage of the buying journey, where you're looking to build an audience and increase website traffic. Examples of appropriate content types here include "quotables" for social media, short videos on social media, and targeted ads and emails with an empathetic tone. Audiograms for social media also work here, which simply describe sound bites (often pulled from podcasts) that are interfaced with some type of video component—a type of content that helps stop the scroll through newsfeeds. Regardless of which type of content you choose here, don't be afraid to lean into pain points a bit and offer your audience hope for a bigger, better, and brighter future.

- **Educating:** this second content archetype is good when you're guiding a consumer from the awareness stage (building an audience to increase website traffic) to the consideration stage of the buying journey. Here, you're looking to attract and generate leads by providing something of value through the sharing of expert insights. Your goal is to help them gain clarity around the questions and concerns holding them back and causing them pain. The way you educate, of course, is through content types like webinars, ask-me-anything videos (where you take common questions and provide answers), ask-me-anything podcasts (which can be two and one of the same, where your audio content is stripped from your video), and finally turning all this video/audio content into blog articles.

- **Empowering:** this is the kind of content archetype we use when we are now looking to nurture those leads coming in. It's where we help people find the courage to really commit and move beyond the concerns holding them back. That commitment starts small at first, for example, as they provide their name and email address in exchange for more premium pieces of content types like e-books, buying guides, checklists, assessments, quizzes, and calculators.

- **Elevating:** finally, as the consumer moves closer to the moment of commitment—when they click the Apply button for a loan or to open an account—the content must move and inspire them. It is here you show how your financial brand has helped others just like them get to their bigger, better, and brighter future. With this content archetype, we use tools like ratings and reviews along with stories of success shared through videos, podcasts, and articles.

> The four archetypes for content production are empathetic, educating, empowering, and elevating.

There's one financial brand we've guided over the years that really comes to mind here. This financial brand took a strategic approach to content marketing as they produced evergreen content libraries that were mapped against digital consumer buying journeys for key product lines. This effort has created exponential value over time.

For example, they used the four content archetypes to develop evergreen content libraries for consumers in the market for an auto loan or mortgage. From there, they also built evergreen content libraries around different life events for when people get married, get divorced, have a baby, or start a business.

This financial brand has also done a great job positioning their small business products by producing and promoting content like their *Small Business Growth Guide*. Just within one week of launching this guide with targeted ads on LinkedIn and Facebook, the financial brand captured a lead that eventually converted into a $15 million commercial loan. Furthermore, the *Small Business Growth Guide* was the start of their annual Small Business Growth Summit they host for businesses in the communities they serve.

Through a continued commitment to *help first and sell second*, this financial brand's evergreen content libraries with a focus on solving problems for consumers have generated tens of thousands of leads over the years. These leads have gone on to convert into loans and deposits generating millions in new income.

For this financial brand, content is not about the random blog or social media post here or there. Instead, content has created value as their marketing and sales teams are guided by a Digital Growth Blueprint and production process that has kept them focused on their goals.

THE DIGITAL GROWTH PILLAR CONTENT PRODUCTION PROCESS

I understand producing evergreen content libraries can feel like an impossible and overwhelming task, especially if you're working with limited resources. But it doesn't have to.

Start your content production journey with the biggest piece of content. This is where a lot of banks and credit unions mess up: they start with the *smallest* piece of content—that is, social content or blog content. They have it backward. You should always begin with the biggest piece of content, whether a guidebook or a video interview.

I'm a big advocate of video. As video content becomes more and more prevalent, we can take all the video being produced, strip out the audio, and then turn the audio into a podcast. This can be done for a solo "ask-me-anything"-like video. It can also be done for a "story of success" interview with a narrative angle, such as one you produce by interviewing an account holder whom your financial brand has helped. You can also take this approach by interviewing some type of subject matter expert either within your own financial brand or another community partner. Point is, you take the video, strip out the audio, and now you have a video *and* a podcast.

Then that video and podcast can, in turn, be the foundation for blog articles. You can also take those videos and podcasts and cut them down to short-form media. The short-form media can become social content you can use to drive traffic back to the articles. Then the articles can also cross-reference e-books and buying guides for download.

As you can see, when you approach content production with a strategic process, content production becomes a much more **methodical and operationally efficient process that generates exponential leads for loans and deposits**, as opposed to a few smattered blog and social posts.

WHAT COMES NEXT

Okay, so you've produced all this great content. Are you familiar with that old expression "If a tree falls in the woods, does anyone hear it?" It's the same idea here. If you produce content but don't *promote* and bring it to market, does it create value?

No, and that's a big problem I see today. Financial brands who are ramping up their content production engine need to also have a content promotion strategy to generate leads through their content marketing efforts.

Again, the definition of content marketing is a well-defined process to produce and promote content. Produce *and promote*. It's that second piece we'll be looking at in the next chapter, with an eye toward both technology and the channels that will serve you best in getting your content marketing out there.

* * * * *

CHAPTER ELEVEN

WE WILL PROMOTE CONTENT ONLY TO GUIDE PEOPLE

When we talk about the brand Red Bull, a lot of people think of only the energy drink. But what Red Bull has actually become over the years is a publishing/media company that is all driven by content.

What they have done through their content, in both their production and especially their promotion, is build an audience—a community—of people who relate to what Red Bull stands for—that is, their purpose.

The Red Bull community is built around the active or extreme lifestyle, BMX, Motor Cross, and so forth. But it's not for everyone. Red Bull has created what is basically its own media publishing arm with magazines and events. Over the course of the brand's successful journey, content has driven everything.

To me, one the greatest and most extreme examples of Red Bull's branded content experiences was in 2012, when Austrian skydiver Felix Baumgartner ascended twenty-four miles above the earth in a helium balloon. As Baumgartner stepped out of his capsule at the edge of space, Red Bull's brand was prominently displayed in almost every single camera shot.

During Baumgartner's record-breaking skydive, YouTube reported more than 8 million concurrent live stream connections. At the time, it was YouTube's biggest live-streamed event to date. Furthermore, Red Bull attributed a 24 percent increase in YouTube subscribers to Baumgartner's jump.[37]

But it hasn't been just the initial production of this event that makes this branded content so effective; it is the ongoing content *promotion* and continuous distribution of that content through multiple channels. Over the years, Red Bull has gone on to maximize the value of this branded content by promoting it multiple ways, including through a BBC documentary, to generate hundreds of millions of views since 2012 while growing their digital community.

What can financial brands learn from the way that Red Bull has promoted and distributed content?

Here's what we have found through our continuous research and studies around the challenges banks and credit unions must overcome when it comes to promoting their content. First, the average financial brand blog post has only twenty-six views. The average financial brand YouTube video has only twenty-two views, and the average traffic driven to a financial brand's website from social media posts is only around 0.1 percent of all website traffic.

---

37 David Lieberman, "YouTube's Red Bull Channel Reports 52M Views for Felix Baumgartner's Space Jump; Discovery Coverage Sets Record," Deadline, August 20, 2019, https://deadline.com/2012/10/felix-baumgartner-red-bull-channel-youtube-views-354667/.

It all begs the question, what's the point? What's the point of the blog content? What's the point of the social media? What's the point of the YouTube videos? Why keep producing content if it doesn't create value?

In fact, there are many times we've recommended financial brands hit the pause button on content production and promotion to focus on other strategic digital growth efforts that create even greater and more proven value. It's important to remember that just like content production, it's important to look at content *promotion* in the context with the digital consumer buying journey.

Traditionally, when we talk about content promotion in the world of financial brands, we think about it only in terms of social media posts. That's the problem. As we're seeing social media continue to mature, it doesn't have the same organic reach as it used to. This is particularly true with Facebook.

I think Facebook has really pulled the wool over a lot of brands—and not just banks and credit unions. Five or ten years ago, the conversations at conferences and through industry publications were about how every brand needed to get on Facebook. As a result, in the years that followed, we saw brands building up their Facebook audiences.

But now, as Facebook has evolved—and has now gone public needing to maximize profits—the organic reach of a Facebook post has fallen to only 2 percent to 6 percent. We spent so much time, effort, energy, and dollars building up our Facebook audiences. But now financial brands have to pay to actually promote their content to that audience.

Think of it this way: if the organic reach of a Facebook post is 6 percent at best, this means that after building an audience of 10,000 people, at best only 600 people may see that post. Or at worse, it will only come across the feed of just 200 people. Is it even worth it at that point to spend time producing that content?

The solution here is that we must pause and rethink our content promotion strategy through the lens of the digital consumer journey.

What we need to focus on are those first three stages of awareness, consideration, and purchase. The future of financial marketing, digital marketing—and really the future of media brands—are all one and the same. They are all built on content promotion through platforms, almost all of which we do not own: key examples include Facebook, Instagram, LinkedIn, Twitter, and YouTube.

In stepping back and reframing how we look at content promotion, we need to view the subject through three different lenses on a spectrum of left to right.

CONTENT **PROMOTION** SPECTRUM

ADS   SOCIAL   EMAIL

BOUGHT   EARNED

On the far left side of the spectrum, we have digital ads, where we're *buying* access to an audience. On the far right side of the spectrum, we have email, where the audience is actually built and *earned* as something we own. We own the email audience.

But in the mushy middle of that spectrum—between bought and earned—sits social media. In theory, social media is organic and therefore earned. But organic reach is failing to such a degree that its impact is almost nominal, which moves social media further to the left on that spectrum, where we're really having to *buy* access to our audience.

PROMOTE CONTENT WITH SOCIAL MEDIA

As social promotion is a natural extension of content production, the following three goals will ensure you maximize the value from the content you produce.

SOCIAL CONTENT PROMOTION GOAL #1: BUY ACCESS TO NICHE AUDIENCES

In today's digital world, just like in the days of broadcast marketing, grabbing and keeping consumers' attention is key to any digital brand building strategy. Consider, on average, consumers spend 2 hours and 23 minutes (that's up from 1 hour and 30 minutes in 2012) scrolling.[38] And it's not just any scrolling; they're maneuvering through scrolling through more than 300 feet of social content every single day.[39]

The signal-to-noise ratio of social media has been exponentially amplified. This is why I highly recommend financial brands budget for paid social content promotion to target niche audiences and ensure the content they produce has a fighting chance to cut through the noise. Organic reach alone will no longer work. Just like in the old days of broadcast marketing, in particular cable media, financial brands paid to access audiences. And what was old—paying to access audiences—is new again. This time, though, with social, the audiences financial brands pay to target and access are more niche and focused, thus having exponentially more relevance to the content produced and promoted.

When compared to the legacy broadcast world of TV and radio, the big difference in today's digital world is that no longer do financial brands have the luxury of running thirty- or sixty-second ad spots to captive broadcast media audiences (hello, Netflix, Hulu, and Spotify). Instead, financial brands now

---

38 Marie Ennis-O'Connor, "How Much Time Do People Spend on Social Media in 2019? [Infographic]," Medium, August 8, 2019, https://medium.com/@JBBC/how-much-time-do-people-spend-on-social-media-in-2019-infographic-cc02c63bede8.

39 NetNewsLedger, "Average Person Scrolls 300 Feet of Social Media Content Daily," NetNewsLedger, June 12, 2019, http://www.netnewsledger.com/2018/01/01/average-person-scrolls-300-feet-social-media-content-daily/.

have just seconds to capture and keep consumer attention. They are not just competing with other brands for attention anymore; they are also competing with memes, cat pictures, the latest viral videos, and whatever else finds its way into the social feed.

Consider for a moment that it takes only 0.25 seconds of content exposure on a mobile device for people to recall branded content at a statistically significant rate. Furthermore, according to Facebook, they have found consumers spend, on average, 1.7 seconds with a piece of content on mobile devices compared to 2.5 seconds on desktops.[40] This reinforces that frequency is key for content promotion through social to be effective, and the only way to frequently promote content is to buy access to audiences with a paid social promotion strategy.

However, we still have to be careful of what we promote: we don't want to continuously promote the same commoditized great rates, amazing service, and so on. The opportunity is to produce and promote content that *helps first and sells second* to position your financial brand as the helpful and empathetic guide.

SOCIAL CONTENT PROMOTION GOAL #2: BUILD YOUR OWN AUDIENCE

If you're investing good money to access niche audiences on social media to promote your content, fully leverage the audience you're targeting by not just promoting content but also building your own audience by generating leads for loans and

---

40 "Capturing Attention in Feed: The Science behind Effective Video Creative," Facebook IQ, accessed December 11, 2019, https://www.facebook.com/business/news/insights/capturing-attention-feed-video-creative.

deposits. It is here you have to be very intentional with the type of content you're promoting on social media to generate leads. Building an audience you own is really just building an email database of prospects who connect with the helpful content you're sharing.

Let's be clear: the content you promote to build your own audience—that is, grow your email database of prospects—cannot be a direct product offer. Instead, you're offering content in regard to the context of where consumers are in the buying journey, all dependent on their unique pains, questions, and concerns. As noted above, for your social content to create value and generate leads for loans and deposits, you must budget to promote the content you produce. Organic reach is dead and is pointless. The good news, according to Financial Brand, is "promoted content generates 21 times more interactions per post than non-promoted content."[41]

To succeed with content promotion and distribution in social media, you really have to pay to play. Some financial brands, like Fifth Third Bank, have paid to promote 75 percent of their content on social media. They're not alone: 95 percent of social media content interactions for BB&T, Capital One, and Regions Bank have been through investing in and paying for promoted content.

Think of the funds you allocate to content promotion like a Hollywood budget. Whenever Hollywood produces a film, at least 50 percent of the production budget is allocated to promotion. We can apply this same type of thinking here. Let's

---

41   *The Financial Brand*, "5 Trends Forcing Financial Marketers to Rethink Social Media Strategy," *The Financial Brand*, October 27, 2017, https://thefinancialbrand.com/68173/social-media-trends-strategy-banking/.

assume your financial brand invests $20,000 to produce a forty-page branded guide to buying a home, landing page with A/B testing of headlines and CTAs, and email marketing automation nurture workflow.

In addition to budgeting for the production of this evergreen content asset, one that will generate leads for years to come, I recommend budgeting at least $10,000 to bring this content to the marketplace to actually *promote* it. You'll do this by placing highly targeted ads on Facebook for those who might be in the market to buy a home. These ads will then drive consumers to a landing page, requiring them to provide their name and email address in exchange for the helpful guide.

In this example, with a total investment of $30,000, all your financial brand needs is likely five to ten mortgages, depending on the sizes of the loans, to break even on this investment through earned net interest income. Any other mortgages you capture from this content asset over the years to come is pure profit, as you'll now have an evergreen mortgage lead generation machine full of content you've successfully produced *and* promoted.

Once again, the end goal of social media is to build an audience we own by leveraging the audiences of social media platforms. This helps us to escape what I call the Zuck Suck. That's the sound you hear when Mark Zuckerberg is sucking all of your dollars to promote your content on Facebook, but all you're getting from it is likes, not leads.

If you're not leveraging social media to build an audience you own by gaining email addresses from leads, then what's the point? What value are you creating with promoting content on social media?

SOCIAL CONTENT PROMOTION GOAL #3: LEVERAGE YOUR TEAM

If organic social content promotion is even going to have a chance, one of the most exciting and untapped opportunities for amplifying that social content is via what I call a SMAG (Social Media Advocacy Group). Here is where you leverage your team's personal accounts—yes, everyone who works for your brand—in an effort to promote the content you're producing through *their own personal* social media channels. Your team members have the potential to be your biggest promoters and advocates on social media. More than that, they *should* be the biggest promoters and advocates of your financial brand on social media.

Think of a SMAG as an exponential social content promotion multiplier. Say, for example, that you have the following:

- 1,000 employees

- 10,000 followers on Twitter

- 30,000 likes on Facebook

- 1,000 followers on LinkedIn

In this case, your current maximum social reach is 41,000. However, with a SMAG, your potential social reach increases by more than 200 percent, to 722,720.

A lot of financial brands hesitate to take this step. They ask me, "Well, how are we going to manage this from a compliance standpoint?" My answer is simple: "It's not that hard." I advise they start small and begin with a pilot program of a select group of staff from different departments. To provide content control, governance, and oversight—while at the same time still leveraging your team member's personal accounts for the promotion of social media—tap into one of many different team social media management platforms, such as like Hootesuite's Amplify—the one, by the way, that we used to complete the reach potential calculation at the beginning of this example.

Bottom line? If you leverage a SMAG, you can see an exponentially larger organic reach than if you just post the content through your corporate channels.

PROMOTING EVERGREEN DIGITAL ADS CREATES EXPONENTIAL VALUE

If content is the fuel of the Digital Growth Engine, then content that is produced can be promoted at every stage of the consumer buying journey through what we call **perpetual evergreen ad campaigns**.

Consumers buy a financial brand product when *they* have a need, not when *you* have a need. When we think about producing and promoting content through the lens of the digital consumer buying journey, the goal is to promote evergreen content assets that create exponential value, literally, for years to come. This provides you with the opportunity to finally break free from the legacy quarterly or monthly marketing campaigns that eventually become a sunk cost. Why? Because once that quarterly campaign is done, those assets are no longer relevant.

The way we look at this is through something that we call the Digital Growth Ad Matrix Method, a six-step process that provides clarity and focus when placing digital ads for each of the first three stages in the buying journey: awareness, consideration, and purchase. Using this tool proactively will help your financial brand avoid losing valuable time, not to mention hundreds of thousands or even millions of ad dollars.

DIGITAL GROWTH AD MATRIX

	AWARENESS	CONSIDERATION	PURCHASE
Define persona question, concern, hope, or dream			
Document type of extrinsic or intrinsic motivation			
Select ad channel			
Write ad headline and copy			
Design ad creative for selected ad channel			
Determine ad KPMs			

The Digital Growth Ad Matrix Method begins with the documentation of consumer personas. In brief review from before, these personas are the ideal representations of your account holders—the profiles of the consumer who might be interested in the products to offer.

Keep in mind here that digital ad campaign personas might not necessarily be the same as the "corporate personas" you've defined to guide your overarching high-level Digital Growth Strategy. These consumer personas are probably going to be a subset of the "corporate personas" and more focused in and around the particular product offering your financial brand is bringing to market. When you're working within the Digital Growth Ad Matrix Method, **persona means the ideal target market for a particular ad campaign**.

Once you've identified the ad campaign persona—which is really tapping into the thick data of their questions, concerns, hopes, and dreams—**the second step of the Digital Growth Ad Matrix Method is to identify the motivations for each persona**. In other words, why would people want to take the next step as you're guiding them through the digital consumer buying journey with your content?

There are two types of motivations your digital ads can address here. One is the extrinsic motivations. These are the factors that relate to someone outside of the self. Typically, there is some type of reward or a tangible object you can tap into. For example, "I want to buy a bigger home to show others how well I'm doing at life." Think of this as like a power play.

Then the intrinsic motivations are the other side of the coin, and they are typically intangible. These, we've found, are even more powerful for your ads to tap into when compared to the extrinsic motivators. Intrinsic motivations are what drive us when we want to do something because of the way it makes us *feel*. They are what give us a sense of joy or hope or purpose. For example, "I want to buy a bigger home so that my family can grow up in a comfortable environment and create lasting memories that we'll share for the rest of our lives."

These motivations are important because they help you see and answer important questions from the perspective of the consumer: *What's in for me? How will you help me? How will I feel? How will I look? How will I live better? How will I be better if I apply for your financial product?*

Extrinsic motivators target more impulsive thinking whereas intrinsic ones target more of the contemplative, long-term perspective and goals. Studies have found that when dealing with complex problems, there's greater value gained by tapping into and targeting intrinsic motivators. As we've noted many times before in this book, money is a very complex matter. What's more, our research has found millennials and other digital natives are naturally more intrinsically motivated as consumers, hence the reason there is power in positioning around a purpose that transcends the promotion of products.

The third step of the Digital Growth Ad Matrix Method is to identify the ad channel you are buying audience access to. There are literally hundreds of different possible traffic sources to choose from, but I recommend sticking to the Big Four to begin with: Google, Facebook/Instagram, LinkedIn, and YouTube. Start by researching your potential audience size as well as the estimated cost to actually reach that audience. Cost will vary greatly depending on geographic location, along with how competitive the product you're promoting is among your intended audience. I recommend starting with and focusing on one single ad channel for your evergreen ad campaign. Then, once you've built a strong foundation, you can add more digital channels to the mix for scale.

The fourth step of the Digital Growth Ad Matrix Method is to write ad copy, including headlines and text. You're going to do this for each of your personas, along with the three different stages of the consumer buying journey. For example, if you start this process with three different personas and you have three different phases of the buying journey, then you have a total of nine different ad headlines and ad copy.

The purpose of this exercise is to begin to create powerful and segmented ads that speak to a particular persona's motivations at every stage of their buying journey. As for the ad headline and copy, those will depend on both the channel and the motivations you're tapping into.

Remember, this is also where the ad content will change. For example, the content offered during the awareness and even consideration stage of the buying journal is likely to be something like an online quiz, assessment, or downloadable consumer buying guide. The ad content offered during the purchase stage will promote content such as a "story of success" video or direct call to action to apply for the loan or open the account.

The fifth step of the Digital Growth Ad Matrix Method is to produce the ad creative. This is where everything comes together. Up to this point, the primary focus of the exercise has been around strategic thinking. Now, instead of just jumping into ad creative, you have a logical and methodical process to make sure the ads you produce are intentional and well thought out.

Your ad creative can include things like videos, pictures, and graphics. All of this will depend on the ad channels you have selected within the Digital Growth Ad Matrix, which, again, is affected by where your target consumer is in their buying journey.

The most important part of the ad creative involves clearly communicating a solution to the consumer persona's questions, concerns, hopes, and dreams. Here, I recommend really leaning into those questions and concerns (the pain points) with your headlines and addressing the intrinsic motivations with your ad copy, ad images, or video.

Again, think of it this way: with your ad, you are offering a cure or anecdote to the consumer's pain and a pathway or solution to help them reach a bigger, better, brighter future.

Finally, **the sixth and last step of this Digital Growth Ad Matrix Method is to measure performance**. You've done all of the work, now it's time to launch the campaigns. Again, if you're targeting three different personas and you have three different stages of the buying journey, that's nine different ads you're going to market with. But you don't know what is going to work until you try it, which is why you have to measure.

After running your ads for five to seven days, you can begin to analyze your results. By tracking your success, you'll have a great sense of what's working, what's not, and how you can optimize your ad campaign going forward to generate even more leads for loans and deposits.

MAXIMIZING EMAIL MARKETING PROMOTION

Finally, a word on email marketing. This is still the work horse of the Digital Growth Engine, and it's where marketing automation comes into play. Econsultancy conducted a study that found email marketing continues to rank as the best digital channel in terms of return on investment. Another study from

Relevancy Group found email alone drives the same amount of revenue as social media and display ad efforts combined.

Yet brands invest only 16 percent of their marketing budget into email!

There is a lot of opportunity here for you to leap ahead of your competition. As you're acquiring leads from either social media or digital ads, use email to nurture these leads and move them from one stage of the buying journey to the next. From our ongoing research, we continue to find this is an untapped opportunity, as 98 percent of financial brands have not deployed a lead nurturing system for the consideration stage of the digital consumer buying journey.

Jupiter Research has also found personalized emails yield significantly better results than nonpersonalized, with personalized emails driving eighteen times more revenue than traditional broadcast emails.

There are two types of emails you can send. The first are targeted emails, and these are traditionally driven by some transaction or product adoption based on the data within your financial brand's core system. The second type are triggered emails, and these are sent based on consumer behavior—behavior on the website or in regard to what's happening through the overall context of your perpetual evergreen digital ad campaigns.

Regardless of whether you're sending targeted or triggered emails, part of your email marketing strategy—really the key—is to A/B test your subject lines. Every email that goes out should have its subject line A/B tested. This is critical because the subject line is what directly impacts whether someone opens the email in the first place. This is also where financial brands can and must use marketing automation to create lists for those targeted email and triggered email sends.

When it comes to email—and if we're looking at email acquisition as the premise of content promotion through both social media as well as digital ads—the whole point is to build an email list to nurture over time. This is why your financial brand's email list is a strategic marketing asset. It has real monetary value. And you must treat it as such.

- - - - -

CHAPTER TWELVE

WE WILL PROVE MARKETING'S VALUE ONCE AND FOR ALL

In chapters ten and eleven, we talked about content production and promotion, respectively. Now, in this final chapter of the book, we are turning our attention to *performance*.

Guiding consumers through the digital consumer buying journey with social content promotion, digital ads, and personalized emails is smart, but none of that matters if you can't measure performance. Otherwise, you're not able to prove what works (and what doesn't). Unfortunately, that's where we stand today with the vast majority of financial brands. It is for this very reason CEOs don't trust financial marketers.

To explain why measuring performance is so important, let me give you a kind of allegory.

There was once a brother and sister. This brother and sister had very different talents, very different skill sets. As they grew up, the brother excelled at math, whereas the sister mastered the arts. Along the way, the brother got all the attention for his grades and academic performance as he went on to become a CFO, whereas the sister's talent for art was ignored and even looked down on.

No one really understood or appreciated her creative thinking, and because she wasn't able to show the impact she made with her art, beyond just paintings and drawings, the sister grew very tired and frustrated. There was no way to *prove* the value she was creating like her CFO brother was able to with his math skills.

Unfortunately, this is exactly what I see happening with financial marketers and marketing teams. Basically, we have these fiefdoms, internal silos. You have the CIO versus the CMO, and the CFO versus the CMO. Traditionally, IT and finance, being very analytical and data driven, have an easier time quantifying both the value and cost reduction coming out of their departments.

Marketing—not so much.

Look, I get it. Traditional broadcast marketing was very hard, if not impossible, to quantify.

This is what led to the perception I've talked about a lot already in this book, where marketing is viewed as a cost center— we put money into it but don't know where it goes or what value it creates. Or worse, marketing is seen as a glorified in-house FedEx Kinko's to serve the last-minute demands of other people. In this kind of climate, marketing teams end up operating in the *doing* environment, and of course they feel overwhelmed—not really making any true progress with what they need to do to become more strategic marketers.

In the worst-case scenario, financial brand marketers are just flat-out disrespected. They're viewed by others as nothing more than kids who play with paint and crayons. A lot of that has to do with the legacy perspective that marketing is a creative profession.

Now, because of digital marketing, that perception is starting to change. Clearly, digital marketing mixes and merges both the analytical and the creative. But the negative images painted by the past are hard to escape. The Fornaise Group conducted a tremendous study that found 80 percent of CEOs don't trust marketers. Meanwhile, 73 percent of CEOs believe marketers lack business credibility and the ability to actually generate growth. On the flip side, 95 percent of CEOs do trust and value the insights of CFOs and CIOs.[42]

According to Jerome Fontaine, CEO and marketing performance chief of the Fornaise Group, "If marketers want to be taken seriously and have a bigger stronger presence in the board room, they need to stop living in their Lala land and start behaving like real business people."[43] Yikes!

That's some tough love, but financial brand marketers need to hear it. Thankfully, it doesn't have to be that way. There is hope, and my ultimate goal for financial marketers is for them to finally, once and for all, prove their value, their worth. How will they do this? By generating 10X more loans and deposits. If they can succeed in this, I guarantee that they will stop feeling like overwhelmed and frustrated order takers.

42   "Marketing Effectiveness News & Releases," Fournaise, accessed December 11, 2019, http://www.fournaisegroup.com/CEOs-Do-Not-Trust-Marketers.asp.

43   "Marketing Effectiveness News & Releases," Fournaise, accessed December 11, 2019, https://www.fournaisegroup.com/76-of-marketers-track-effectiveness-wrongly/.

I've seen it happen time and time again. They become the strategic leader executive teams respect, value, and trust to guide *them* toward a bigger, better, brighter future of exponential digital growth. That's my hope with all of this.

So how do we do it? There are three steps to measure and improve digital growth.

First, we need to establish three foundational numbers that will help us answer the essential questions: How much is a new account worth to us? How much is a loan worth to us? How much is a credit card worth to us?

THREE FOUNDATIONAL NUMBERS

How Much Is a New Account, Loan, or Credit Card Worth to You?

ACCOUNT

Average Customer
Lifetime Value

LOAN

Average Net
Interest Income

CREDIT CARD

Average Credit Card
Profitability

The three important numbers here are average customer lifetime value for a new account, average net interest income for all our different loan products, and finally, average credit card holder profitability.

If we can establish these foundational numbers—and it's going to require some conversations and maybe even a little negotiation with your CFO to get him or her to commit to ballpark figures—then you can back your way into the information you're really trying to gather, the value of a new account, loan, and credit card.

Armed with this new information, you'll not only then be able to see the value your digital marketing campaigns are creating at the point of conversion, but you can also begin to put together a full funnel analysis where you see the value in each product pipeline mapped to the different stages of the digital consumer journey.

Specifically, after you've established your three foundational numbers, the second step is for you to close the loop. This is one of the biggest strategic pain points for financial brands on a Digital Growth Journey today. In our research, we've found that 89 percent of financial brands do not have a full funnel, closed loop marketing reporting system. Obviously, that's a huge problem because it's impossible to know how the digital marketing is performing beyond vanity metrics.

That's what we're trying to fix here. Our analytics, our reporting, has to move beyond vanity metrics. This is the classic problem with financial brand marketers: whenever they do report metrics from their digital marketing, it is vanity metrics, things like clicks, likes, shares, and follows. But your CEO and CFO don't care about that stuff. What they want to know is what did you get from your digital marketing efforts in relation to leads generated, loans booked, deposits acquired, and new accounts gained. That's it!

Therefore, until your financial brand marketing team can close that loop, you're still going to be viewed as cost centers, glorified in-house FedEx Kinko's, or kids playing with paint and crayons. Again, it doesn't have to be that way—and that's why traditionally I've recommended fixing the conversion problem first.

This is why measurement is such a problem in the first place. There's not a good system for tracking conversions. Whenever someone goes to apply for a loan or open up a new account, they are sent off to a third-party website for their application—and that's where the analytical tracking system breaks down.

How do we solve this problem? With what we call the Digital Growth Closed Loop Conversion Method. This method provides insights into how digital marketing channel performance is happening within the context of conversion points for loans and deposits. It measures the effectiveness of each channel and ultimately allows you to measure conversion beyond just the application. For example, you may have conversion points for thresholds like requesting a callback, downloading a consumer buying guide, or completing an assessment or quiz. Those don't necessarily tell the whole story, but they do give you the ability to put together a picture of the entire funnel—from awareness and consideration to purchase—when you also tie in landing page visits and ad clicks for an evergreen digital ad campaign.

I also recommend closing the loop with marketing automation rule sets. This is a wise thing to do because the data obtained by these conversions can then be utilized for remarketing of abandoned applications under both proactive email and ad campaigns.

Now, if a financial brand doesn't have a marketing automation system in place, they can certainly use Google Analytics as a fallback. This provides another path for that closed loop conversion.

The problem, however, is once again 85 percent to 90 percent of financial brands lack either of these capabilities. It's crazy: performance measurement is where the greatest value is created. It's where marketers can learn, understand, and finally prove what works to generate loans and deposits. But they lack the tools or the knowledge, or just haven't done it for one reason or another.

That is what this chapter—and, in many ways, this whole book—is trying to change.

Toward that end, the last thing we have to do to measure digital growth and prove our worth as financial brand marketers is to establish dashboards. Now that we have these benchmark foundational numbers in regard to what a new account is worth to us, what a loan is worth to us, and what a credit card is worth to us, how do we keep track of all the data that is going to be coming through?

Digital marketing campaigns generate a ton of data that can be complex, confusing, and overwhelming. And all of this data must be tied back to revenue. **Data is the means for measuring ROI and effectiveness, but that doesn't mean data is actually easy to understand.**

Today, financial brand marketers have access to more performance data than ever before. The problem is that it's inaccessible to most people because the data lives in so many different places, behind different platforms, different apps, different systems, different logins, and different passwords.

Just that distribution of data alone makes everyone's job that much harder. It's also why it's so hard to communicate the value of your financial brand's marketing team and the important work you're doing to other key stakeholders.

In fact, it's not uncommon for marketers to use a dozen different tools: third-party apps, backend systems, analytical platforms, and more. It all just gets dumped into these manual, very elaborate Excel spreadsheets that are designed to track performance on different levels.

But these only give us a cursory understanding of how marketing is connecting with business goals. Here's the key point. **Insights cannot be obtained without analytics, and analytics are dead without data.** When you're working within all these third-party systems, you're really piecemealing the data together. You're probably taking screenshots, downloading CSV files, copying and pasting data from one element to the next, utilizing spreadsheets and slide decks.

By the time the data is "visualized" and presented to others, it's probably already outdated. It's too late then to make any kind of informed decisions or take action based on the insights.

Here, again, is where financial brand marketing teams get stuck in the present because they're making decisions that are actually and literally informed by the past. Think of it this way: If you were flying an airplane, your decisions would be informed by your control panel, your dashboard. What if you could see data on the dashboard only a week or even a month later? Not very reassuring! But that's what happens with reporting when it comes to financial brand marketing teams.

That's why real-time dashboards are so important. Your Digital Growth Dashboard pulls data from multiple sources

(Facebook, YouTube, Google AdWords, Google Analytics, Marketing Automation) and then displays it in a single location.

In a glance, you can see how your full funnel evergreen ad campaigns are performing. It provides a single source of truth for your marketing, sales, and leadership teams alike and allows your bank or credit union to drill down into data for deeper investigation and insights as needed.

Furthermore, this is where AI and automation can help set up proactive alerts and notifications within your dashboards based on performance settings. Think of this like the alerts on a plane. You can actually get these alerts ahead of time to inform you if you're either gaining or losing altitude and then adjust as needed to ensure you're making forward progress along your Digital Growth Journey.

Digital Growth Dashboards can save the day while also elevating marketing to the position it deserves: as the strategic leader to guide your financial brand along a journey toward exponential digital growth.

CONCLUSION

COMMIT TO MOVE FORWARD WITH COURAGE AND CONFIDENCE

Digital growth is a journey.

A journey from good to great.

At the Digital Growth Institute, we are on a mission to simplify digital marketing and sales strategies that empower financial brands to generate 10X more loans and deposits.

We do this through the Digital Growth Method that provides clarity for financial brand marketing, sales, and leadership teams as they gain the systems, technologies, and habits they need to maximize their digital growth potential.

As a result, leadership teams no longer feel confused and frustrated about future growth as our research and insights elevate their marketing and sales teams to confidently guide 10X more people in the communities they serve beyond financial stress toward a bigger, better, and brighter future.

We do all of this because money *is* stressful. This stress takes a toll on people's health, their relationships with friends and family, and their overall sense of well-being.

But it doesn't have to be this way!

Commit to rise above the commoditized promotion of dollars and cents to transform the lives of people in the communities you serve through your financial brand's digital marketing and sales strategies. As a result, you *will* generate 10X more loans and deposits.

GET READY TO RUN THE GOOD RACE

Digital growth is like running a marathon. It starts with proper training and planning. And once you start running, it requires you to be open to changing conditions as the environment is unpredictable.

As you should know by now, the good news is that you don't have to run this race alone.

I understand it's easy to quickly feel overwhelmed and frustrated as digital continues to change the world at an exponential pace. Trying to digest what's going on in the world of digital growth might feel like you have to eat this giant whale—an impossible feat.

The good news? It's not impossible. There is a lot to learn from Melinda Mae, a little girl featured in a poem by Shel Silverstein, who appears to be *literally* tasked with eating a whale. What does she do, then? Silverstein writes, in part, "She thought she could/She said she would/So she started right in at the tail."

Spoiler alert: in the end, she gets the job done. So whenever you feel a bit overwhelmed and frustrated about digital growth, remember little Melinda Mae, and let's eat this digital whale together bite by bite by bite.

To begin, commit to using the Digital Growth Strategic Marketing Manifesto as a guide to help you and your team gain clarity, progress with focus, and excel in your Digital Growth Journey.

Start your journey by blocking out time to break free from "doing digital" and begin "thinking digital." Start small and commit to one hour per week. Then one hour every three days. Go all the way until you work your way up to blocking out one day a week to simply think about your digital growth strategy.

DEFINE YOUR ANNUAL DIGITAL GROWTH BLUEPRINT

Use the Digital GROWTH Blueprint strategic framework below to guide your thinking, as this will help to increase your team's courage to commit to move forward.

- **Goals:** What are your goals for growth? Let's assume you and I are having cocktails or coffee twelve months from now, and I ask you what's been going on over the past year. You have a big smile on your face as you think about all you've done to reach this good place. Yes, here you are leaping ahead two years in your mind and looking backward. Ask yourself: What has to happen between now and then for you to feel good about the progress you've made along your Digital Growth Journey? Be as specific and detailed as possible, as this is where you begin to create your own bigger, better, and brighter future. Now come back to the present moment, and let's work through some more questions.

- **Roadblocks:** What roadblocks or challenges do you see today that must be eliminated over the next twelve months for you and your financial brand to make progress along your Digital Growth Journey?

- **Opportunities:** What new opportunities do you see that you can create or capture? What strengths do you have today that you can maximize over the next twelve months as your financial brand continues to make progress along your Digital Growth Journey?

- **Who before How:** Who do you need to work together with to eliminate your roadblocks while empowering you to capture the opportunities you have identified above?

- **Tools:** What specific tools and technologies do you need to acquire, or further maximize, to continue to make progress along your Digital Growth Journey over the next twelve months?

- **How:** What specific steps and actions must you commit to take to ensure you begin to move forward and make progress on your Digital Growth Journey?

I recommend this strategic activity be done every twelve months at a high level. In addition, review and optimize every ninety days as you continue to make progress.

That is the key: focus on progress. Measure your success by looking behind at where you've come from instead of looking ahead at where you want to go. As you look behind day after day, week after week, month after month, you and your team's confidence will continue to increase as you break free from legacy marketing and sales systems built around branches and broadcast.

As a result, you'll stop feeling confused, frustrated, and overwhelmed about digital growth. Because working together with your team, your financial brand will confidently generate 10X more loans and deposits as you guide people in the communities you serve beyond their financial stress toward a bigger, better, and brighter future.

SIGN THE DIGITAL GROWTH MANIFESTO

(Tip: take the next page, tear it out, frame it, and put it where you can see it every single day.)

I will help _____ maximize our digital growth potential as we generate 10X more loans and deposits by guiding people in the communities we serve beyond their financial stress toward a bigger, better, and brighter future.

To do this, I commit to always:

Learn from the past to escape the present.

Define a Digital Growth Purpose.

Empathize with consumer personas.

Position products beyond bullet points.

Escape the dangers of doing digital.

Map out digital consumer journeys.

Maximize marketing technologies.

Build a website that sells.

Be the helpful and empathetic guide.

Produce content that helps first and sells second.

Promote content only to guide people.

Prove marketing's value once and for all.

X_____

ACKNOWLEDGMENTS

The real reason you are reading this book right now is because on February 11, 2002, when I was a sophomore in college, a girl in the library told me to quit my punk rock band and do something with my life. She was brutally honest as she shared how bad she thought my band sucked; she was right.

I liked this girl and wanted nothing more than to impress her. So I listened to her brutal, harsh, and honest truth as she called me to take action—to be better. On that same day, I sold my band equipment, went down to the courthouse and got a DBA, and started what would grow and become the Digital Growth Institute. At the time, I had no idea how to grow a business. It was harder than I ever imagined.

The good news is that four years later, this girl and I got married. She truly has been with me every step of the way on this journey from the very beginning. And as we have gone through the ups and downs of both marriage and business, we have celebrated the highest of highs while also crying together in our lowest lows.

My bride has stayed by my side over the years—on countless late nights when we both should have been in bed asleep together—while I researched and typed away into the early morning hours. She has also held down the fort far too many times to count with our four small children at home when I've been on the road traveling and speaking. I am truly thankful she has given me both the support and opportunity to do important and meaningful work I enjoy.

My wife is my best friend. A woman of valor, wisdom, and noble character. God's blessing to me. An angel without wings. My helpful guide. She is an amazing mother to our four beautiful children. Her strength and courageous spirit inspire and challenge me to always be an even better husband, father, author, speaker, and advisor. And to this day, I am grateful she is not afraid to speak the brutal, harsh, and honest truth or call me to action—even when I don't want to hear it—as she is most likely protecting me from myself.

That's why I want to acknowledge and thank my wife, Delena, for truly being my helpful and empathetic guide on this journey. I love her dearly, and I am forever grateful for the unending support, patience, and grace she has shared with me as we work together to create a bigger, better, and brighter future for our family and those around us.

First and foremost, you are reading this book right now because of Delena.

But getting this book out of my head and onto these pages would not be possible without my amazing publishing team at Scribe Media and the Digital Growth Institute.

Just like it takes a village to raise a child, it also takes a village to bring a book to life. From the first time I sat down and chatted with JT McCormick and Rikki Jump when I was speaking at a banking conference in Austin, I knew I was in good hands and that this book would finally get out of my head and become reality. Big thanks to my publishing manager, Donnie McLohon, for keeping things on track and moving forward every step of the way. I also appreciate and am grateful for my scribe, Mark Chait, and all of the patience and guidance he shared with me throughout the writing process. Thanks to Cindy Curtis and the entire design team for the cover art—a picture really is worth a thousand words—as well as to Amanda Kelly and Gennipher Dudot for keeping me on task and focused so I could follow through and actually get this thing done.

Finally, I would like to thank you, dear reader, for taking time to read this book and joining me on my quest to transform financial brand marketing and sales strategies that guide people beyond the financial stress that takes a toll on their health, their relationships with friends and family, and their overall sense of well-being. Working together, we can all guide 10X more people in the communities we live and work in toward a bigger, better, and brighter future.

ABOUT THE AUTHOR

JAMES ROBERT LAY is one of the world's leading digital marketing authors, speakers, and advisors for financial brands. As the founder and CEO of the Digital Growth Institute, he has guided more than 520 financial brands on a mission to simplify digital marketing strategies that empower banks and credit unions to generate 10X more loans and deposits. His insights have been featured in outlets including *U.S. News & World Report*, *The Financial Brand*, *American Banker*, *Credit Union Times*, and *Credit Union Journal*. James Robert has also spoken at 200+ events and leads the CUES School of Strategic Marketing while lecturing at universities throughout the United States.

Made in the USA
Coppell, TX
08 March 2021

51436574R00164